The Couple Who Fell in Hate

And Other Tales of Eclectic Psychotherapy

by

Gerald Schoenewolf, Ph.D.

JASON ARONSON INC.
Northvale, New Jersey
London

The author gratefully acknowledges permission to reprint the following:

Chapter 2, "Buttons," from *Voices: The Art and Science of Psychotherapy* 30(4), Winter 1994, copyright © 1994 American Academy of Psychotherapists and Guilford Press. Used by permission of the American Academy of Psychotherapists.

Chapter 8, "The Couple Who Fell in Hate," from *The Journal of Contemporary Psychotherapy*, Spring 1996, copyright © 1996.

Production Editor: Elaine Lindenblatt

This book was set in 11 point Garamond by TechType of Ramsey, New Jersey, and printed and bound by Book-mart Press of North Bergen, New Jersey.

Library of Congress Cataloging-in-Publication Data

Schoenewolf, Gerald.
    The couple who fell in hate : and other tales of eclectic psychotherapy
    / by Gerald Schoenewolf.
        p.   cm.
    Includes bibliographical references and index.
    ISBN 1-56821-746-3
    1. Electic psychotherapy—Case studies.   I. Title.
    RC489.E24S36   1996
    616.89'14—dc20   95-32110

Manufactured in the United States of America. Jason Aronson Inc. offers books and cassettes. For information and catalog write to Jason Aronson Inc., 230 Livingston Street, Northvale, New Jersey 07647.

To David Belgray and Jeff Seinfeld

CONTENTS

PREFACE

From the beginnings of psychoanalysis, case histories have been utilized to illustrate theoretical material. Along the way, the genre of the literary case history was born. Freud himself started this trend with "Little Hans," which brims with sparkling dialogue. Many others have since made lasting contributions, including Groddeck (*The Book of the It*), Binswanger (*The Fall of Ellen West*), and Lindner (*The Fifty-Minute Hour*).

In this volume I am using the literary case history not only to illuminate various character types, but primarily to illustrate my particular approach to eclectic psychotherapy. There has been a movement in the field today toward eclectic psychotherapy and away from the more narrowly focused therapies of the past. However, there continues to be a gap between psychoanalysts and nonanalytic therapists. Many psychoanalysts still look askance at nonanalytic techniques, and many nonanalytic therapists question the validity of psychoanalysis. Hence, while many therapists today are eclectic, their eclecticism is nevertheless limited to either psychoanalytic or nonanalytic techniques.

The present volume combines both kinds of interventions and is an organized overview of an eclectic approach. Part I briefly explains the rationale for such an approach and describes how a basic psychoanalytic framework is integrated with Gestalt, behavioral, expressive, mirroring, and joining techniques. Part II contains eight "tales" which demonstrate—engagingly, I hope—how through the years these techniques have been formulated and used in therapy.

I thank the patients, both those who have agreed to have their cases reported here (in disguise) and others who have contributed to the development of eclectic techniques.

PART I

RATIONALE

CHAPTER 1

Overview of Eclectic Psychotherapy

THE FORERUNNERS

In the beginning there was Freud, and Freud said to his patients, "Tell me everything that comes into your mind without censoring," and he saw that it was good, and he called it "the basic rule."

And then Freud listened to his patients and he heard what they were saying below what they were saying, and he said, "That is your unconscious, of which I am proud." And then he said, "All the days of your psychoanalysis I will make what was unconscious conscious."

And then Freud heard the unconscious of his patients and he told them the meaning of what he heard, and afterward they knew that they were naked, and he said "Meanings are good," and he called them "interpretations."

And then Freud said to his patients, "Tell me your dreams," and he listened to their dreams and he saw that dreams were also good, and he told his patients the meanings of their dreams and he called this "dream interpretation."

And then Freud made one of his patients fall asleep

*and she sat up in her sleep and clung to him and wanted
to know him and it was all right: he called it the "erotic
transference." But at that moment a servant walked in
and called it something else, and Freud jumped away
from the patient and saw that it was bad, and he
awakened her from her slumber, and henceforth he sat
behind her and other patients and no longer put them
into a sleep. He then commanded that his followers do
likewise, saying to them, "Cursed be the man who shall
eat of the tree of active therapy."*

*And it came to pass that Freud's method was called
"the standard procedure," of which he was proud, and he
proclaimed that any technique that deviated from the
standard procedure was bad, and he called such devia-
tions, "wild analysis."*

If there were a gospel about the beginnings of psychoanalysis, perhaps it would go something like this. Despite
being an experimenter and an eclectic therapist himself,
Freud maintained a narrow view of how psychoanalytic
therapy would be conducted. In a way, he was like a
parent who says, "Do as I say, not as I do." For his
followers, he strongly advocated that they stick to his
basic procedure, which was set forth in a series of papers
(Freud 1900, 1910, 1912, 1914, 1915, 1916–1917, 1926,
1937), almost like a set of Freudian commandments:

1. The patient shall come five or six times a week.
2. The patient shall lie on a couch.
3. The therapist shall sit behind the couch.
4. The patient shall free associate.
5. The patient shall bring in dreams.
6. The therapist shall interpret, making conscious
   what was formerly unconscious.

7. The therapist shall remain abstinent, and shall in no way gratify the patient or himself.
8. The therapist shall remain neutral, like a blank screen, revealing nothing about his own personal thoughts or feelings.
9. The therapist shall remain passive, never initiating anything but only responding to the material presented by the patient.
10. The therapist shall hold all that the patient says as confidential.

However, Freud himself often deviated from these "commandments." For example, he lent money to the Wolf Man, ordered him not to see a certain woman at the beginning of his therapy, and set a premature termination of his therapy in order to try to break an impasse (Freud 1918). He served herring to the Rat Man, recommended a book for him to read, and asked to see a picture of the Rat Man's girlfriend (Freud 1909). He apparently broke the confidentiality rule by communicating with Dora's father about her treatment (Freud 1905).

But through the years it was recognized by even the most orthodox psychoanalysts that there was a need for a widening scope of analysis. Adler (1929), Ferenczi (1933), and Reich (1933) were the first to experiment with more eclectic techniques. Adler stressed a behaviorialist and family-centered approach; Ferenczi and Reich utilized more active techniques in treating disturbed patients. Although Freud frowned on such experiments and labeled them "wild analysis," they persisted.

Not until Eissler's (1953) famous paper on parameters did the orthodox psychoanalytic community finally recognize that standard procedure simply did not work with many, if not most, patients—at least not in the beginning of therapy. In this paper Eissler suggests that in treating

more disturbed patients (addictive, narcissistic, borderline, or schizophrenic personalities), an analyst might
deviate from the standard procedure and use "parameters"—that is, nonanalytic techniques—but only when
necessary. And he cautioned that such parameters must be
used very carefully, with the patient being notified that
such a deviation was being employed and was only a
temporary measure. By that time, numerous therapists,
both inside and outside of psychoanalysis, had developed
alternative techniques for the array of patients who came
for treatment, and the overwhelming gasp of such therapists was, "It's about time."

Since then, numerous professionals have contributed to
the arsenal of eclectic therapy. Winnicott (1949) coined
the terms *objective hate* and *subjective hate* and demonstrated how a therapist could use confrontation, mirroring, and emotional communication. Fromm-Reichmann
(1950), Searles (1965), Rosen (1962), and Laing (1971) led
the way to a more eclectic treatment of schizophrenics. M.
Erickson (Haley 1973) developed a repertoire of hypnotic,
behavioral, and paradoxical joining and mirroring techniques and focused on the family milieu. Perls (1969)
formulated an existential, active technique. Kohut (1971),
Spotnitz (1976), and Kernberg (1975) devised joining,
mirroring, and confrontative techniques for narcissistic
and borderline patients. Lowen (1958) extended Reichian
therapy, using physical exercises to undo repression and
bring about awareness. Numerous others have made contributions.

THE BASIC FRAMEWORK

I have borrowed from all of these people in developing my
own brand of eclectic psychotherapy. Not all of them

were psychoanalysts, however, and some of their techniques are considered not to be compatible with analysis. For example, behavioral therapy, which does not believe insight is necessary for change, is thought by many analysts not to be compatible with psychoanalysis, which makes insight the key to change. Hence my form of eclecticism differs from most.

The basic premise of my system of eclectic psychotherapy is that standard procedure represents a framework upon which therapy is built. Each patient has particular needs, and each therapy relationship evolves in its own particular way. Hence, the treatment plan must be virtually custom designed for each patient and redesigned moment by moment as the therapy develops. Often in the beginning and early middle stages of treatment a slew of nonanalytic techniques must be used. However, eventually a therapy relationship comes down to the analysis of transference and resistance. Only when this is done will the patient truly understand firsthand how he or she is operating in self-destructive ways.

This is not to say that nonanalytic approaches are ineffective in and of themselves. I cannot evaluate the success or failure of other approaches, and I would not put too much importance on such an evaluation. The personality of the therapist remains the most important variable in the treatment, not his or her technique. Even Freud (1912) admitted that although his technique was the one that worked best for him, it was not necessarily a technique that would be right for other therapists, whose contributions differed from his. Of course, Freud did not mean that a therapist with a paranoid personality should feel free to develop a therapy of paranoia. There are limits to eclecticism.

The therapy relationship begins with the setting up of a psychoanalytic framework. I ask my patients to lie on the

couch and I sit behind them. This sets up a formalized
ritual and creates a serious tone. It also aids objectivity if
the patient and therapist are not making eye contact and
are each freed to ponder without such distraction. Many
patients resist the couch. They are afraid of becoming
controlled and dependent, afraid of being infantilized,
afraid of losing their minds. They want to be on equal
terms with the therapist, as friends or buddies. They want
to keep their eyes on the therapist, make sure he does not
go to sleep. All of these represent resistances related to
events in their childhood within their original primary
relationships.

There are two stages of therapy—the stage of socialization and the stage of analysis. In the beginning and middle
part of the therapy, patients must be "socialized." Sometimes patients will insist on sitting up for a while, will
come late, will forget to pay, or will resist in other ways.
A host of eclectic techniques must be used before the
patient is ready to settle down and work cooperatively
with the therapist. The process of socialization may go on
for days, weeks, or years, depending on the severity of the
disturbance. In effect, the therapist must do the work of
socializing that the parent neglected. Eventually, however, the patient comes around to standard procedure.

The singular, irreplaceable aspect of psychoanalytic
therapy is its stress on using the therapy relationship itself
as a model of change. Patients can talk about relationships
outside, but their relationship with their therapist is immediate. Looking at how they are transferring things onto
their therapist and resisting intimacy and cooperation
with him is an essential, if not key, part of any treatment.
It confronts patients head-on with what they are doing,
not only in their therapy relationship but also in all others.

For the most part, day in and day out, I use standard
procedure. Eclectic techniques are thrown in only to

attend to impasses and treatment-destructive resistances. When I use nonanalytic procedures, I generally tell patients that I am throwing in a nonanalytic technique and explain why it is being used.

GESTALT TECHNIQUES

My first training was as a Gestalt therapist. I tried to use Gestalt techniques exclusively with all my patients and soon found that I was losing many of them. Gestalt is one of the most active of techniques, and I found that if I used it exclusively patients stopped responding to it, as though I had overused some kind of medication. Then they became threatened by therapy itself.

In the beginning, patients generally want to please their therapist and will enthusiastically do the exercises. However, after a while, they feel controlled by the therapist and their resistance increases; active technique then becomes a counterresistance. And since, in this kind of atmosphere, analysis of transference and resistance is not stressed, it is not adequately dealt with. The feelings beneath the resistance build up until the patient cannot tolerate them anymore and either resists more or quits altogether.

However, I have used Gestalt exercises successfully with patients who need to be grounded in the present or need to vent feelings. These include suicidal personalities, addictive personalities, borderlines, and dissociated types. I demonstrate the use of a Gestalt, directed questioning approach with a borderline epileptic patient in Chapter 2, and various Gestalt and behavioral techniques with a multiple personality in Chapter 6.

Gestalt exercises—like all the eclectic techniques to be

described here—can be either straightforward or paradoxical. In straightforward Gestalt, the therapist gives the patient an exercise that has a direct aim—to get the patient more in touch with a particular thought or feeling. Paradoxical exercises are designed to achieve an aim opposite to what they would seem to be pointed toward, in order to get the patient in touch with more strongly defended or repressed material.

Straightforward

Straightforward Gestalt basically consists of the therapist's devising exercises that are designed to enhance the patient's awareness of the here-and-now. For example, if a patient has a headache, you may ask him to give his headache a voice. "What does your headache say?" By speaking from the pain in the head, the patient may suddenly get in touch with the conflict that is causing the headache. "My headache says, 'Stop squashing me!' " the patient may say. The therapist asks, "Who's squashing you?" The patient may say, "My husband."

Similarly, you may have a patient give voice to all people and even things in a dream. Hence he may speak for himself, for the naked stranger, and may even give a voice to the clouds in the sky or to the black hole in the ground. "I'm saying, 'Stay away from me!' and the naked stranger is saying, 'I can't stay away, I'm you—I'm your wildness' and the clouds are saying, 'Don't you dare,' and the black hole is saying, 'You can crawl inside me and stay warm.' " Hence, the meaning of the dream takes on a dynamic, not just intellectual, form.

Or you can have a patient act out a conflict, say, between his id (internalized child) and his superego (internalized authority figure). "As my child, I say, 'I need a hug, oh, please, please, give me a hug. In fact, I need a thousand hugs. Oh, my, I'm so lonely.' As my superego, I say, 'Don't be such a wimp. Get on with your life.' And so I—my ego—is paralyzed. I can neither ask for a hug nor move on.''

Paradoxical

A patient who is in denial may give his headache a voice by saying, "I don't care about my wife anymore. I couldn't care one way or another." Knowing that the anger and hurt is being denied, the therapist says, "Keep saying, 'I don't care.' " The patient repeats it. "Say it louder," the therapist commands. As the patient exaggerates his denial, he begins to get in touch with the anger behind it. Before long he is shouting, "But I *do* care!"

Gestalt techniques are useful during times of crisis, when patients are overwhelmed by emotions, confused, anxious, or disoriented, and they need immediate relief.

BEHAVIORAL TECHNIQUES

Behavioral techniques are necessary in working with phobics, addictives, and perverse patients, and useful with other types in certain situations (see Chapters 4 and 8, and Table 1–1).

Behavioral techniques can include hypnosis (using either formal or informal induction), confrontation (confronting a phobia about elevators by taking the patient onto an elevator), assignments (breaking an addiction by having the patient write down every time he or she eats a cookie or smokes a cigarette), or changing an individual's environment or circumstances (having a parent change a child's home or school environment).

Table 1–1
Eclectic Techniques and Patient Types

Gestalt Techniques	Suicidal personalities, hysterics, borderlines, addictives, obsessives
Behavioral Techniques	Phobics, perverts, addictives, dissociatives, suicidal personalities, obsessives
Mirroring Techniques	Narcissists, perverts, borderlines, schizophrenics, sociopaths, pathogenic personalities, dissociatives, depressives, manic-depressives
Joining Techniques	Narcissists, schizophrenics, depressives, paranoids, traumatized personalities
Expressive Techniques	Hysterics, borderlines, schizophrenics, manic-depressives (artists), dissociatives

Straightforward

I rarely use formal hypnosis anymore, although patients frequently ask me to hypnotize them. This desire to be hypnotized is generally linked to a need for merger (often harkening to the stage of symbiosis), to be taken care of like an infant, and to absolve themselves of the responsibility of probing their own psyches. I do use informal induction with certain types—for instance, with addictive or perverse patients (another type of addiction), who often need some kind of hypnotic, repetitive chant to break down the gristle of pregenital dependency that underlies their addiction (see Chapter 4). I will often think up assignments for patients to help them break an addiction or impasse, as when I assigned a depressed man with a sleep disorder the task of keeping a notebook beside his bed and writing down all his thoughts at the times he could not sleep. This task not only produced interesting material to talk about in our sessions, it also became such a labor for him that he preferred to go to sleep rather than to search his tormented mind and write its contents in the notebook.

Paradoxical

M. Erickson (Haley 1973) was noted for a paradoxical behavioral approach. For example, a mother complained to him that her daughter refused to leave the house because she was so self-conscious about having big feet. Erickson went to the house, pretending to attend to the mother's "fever." While standing over the mother's bed, he "accidentally" (on purpose) stepped on the daughter's foot, and yelled at her, "Why don't they grow those things big enough so a man can see them!" The daughter ran off in horror, but reportedly trotted to school the next day and had no further self-consciousness about her feet.

This was a behavioral approach because he did something to shape her behavior, and it did not depend upon her gaining insight. It was paradoxical in that while he seemed to have been hurting her, he was actually helping her. He understood that big feet symbolize "a big penis" and that she suffered from a castration complex, but he did not need to tell her that. Erickson's cases sound spectacular, since he seems to achieve great success without long-term therapy. My own experience is that paradoxical behavioral procedures may get rid of an impasse or symptom, but that follow-up psychodynamic therapy is still needed to change deeply ingrained characterological patterns.

MIRRORING TECHNIQUES

Like behavioral techniques, those of mirroring can also be either straightforward or paradoxical. Straightforward mirroring is useful for narcissistic, perverse, dissociative, or schizophrenic personalities. Paradoxical mirroring is often necessary in treating borderlines, sociopaths, depressives, and manic-depressives.

When I think of mirroring, I think of the queen in *Snow White and the Seven Dwarfs,* who used to stare in a mirror and say, "Mirror, mirror, on the wall, who's the fairest of them all?" The mirror was expected to "mirror" her as she wanted to be seen. When it didn't, when it said that Snow White was the fairest in the land, the queen flew into a vindictive rage.

Straightforward

The queen is an example of a narcissistic personality. When such personalities first enter therapy, and sometimes for years afterward, they need to be mirrored by the therapist. The therapist must appear to think and act just as the patient does. Kohut (1971) called this a twinship transference. Perverse patients and addictives (who have a healthy degree of narcissism) also have a need for the therapist to mirror them. They want to think that the therapist has or once had the same urges as they have, and the therapist must be willing to lean a little in their direction in the early going in order to build trust.

Alcoholics almost invariably ask me, when they start therapy, if I have ever had a drinking or drug problem. They want to know that I can truly understand them. I usually say, "I've had my own addictions and overcome them." A narcissistic individual, say an artist who needs to feel that he is a talented genius (when he has turned out only a handful of mediocre works), who harbors the notion that he is superior to all the peasants out there, will need me to mirror this in the beginning. When he looks into my eyes, he expects the mirror to say, "Yes, yes, you are the fairest artist in all the land." I must go along with this for a while, until his ego has been strengthened enough so that he can tolerate reality. In reality he may well have talent, but the talent will be undermined by the pressure he puts on himself to be an immediate reincarnation of Da Vinci, as well as by rage toward primary figures toward which he is compensating and with which he has not dealt.

Paradoxical

Paradoxical mirroring is often essential for acting out types—borderlines, sociopaths, pathogenic personalities (see Chapters 3, 7, and 9). In paradoxical mirroring, the therapist may act out in the same way the patient is acting out, but exaggerate it for effect. When a patient came to me several weeks in a row asking me how long he should put up with me as a therapist, I began countering by asking him how long he thought I ought to put up with him as a patient. At first he tried to laugh it off, saying, "You're just trying to use reverse psychology." But when I persisted for weeks to counter him in this way, and was dead serious about it, he got the message and desisted asking this question.

Straightforward mirroring is a holding operation. Paradoxical mirroring is a slap in the face, a "Thanks, I needed that" kind of intervention. It forces the patient to own what he or she has been projecting onto the therapist.

JOINING TECHNIQUES

Joining is useful during the early stages for most severely disturbed types—including narcissistic, schizophrenic, and paranoid personalities, and for sufferers of posttraumatic stress and those going through mourning (see Chapters 4 and 5).

Straightforward

Straightforward joining is used for patients whose reality-testing operation of their ego has been damaged by a family milieu that made the patient confused. A young female patient used to continually express hate for her parents, who had truly abused her, and then she would say to me, "But maybe I shouldn't hate them. Maybe my perceptions are all wrong, as they keep telling me." I would always join her in hating her parents saying, "Your parents were truly hateful. Not on purpose. They meant well. They thought they were just giving you normal discipline. But actually they were being quite hateful." In another case, a young man needed me to join him with regard to quitting a job. He wanted to quit, even though he did not have any other form of employment. I feared if he quit his job he would be continuing a repeating pattern and jeopardizing his therapy, since he would not be able to afford it. Nevertheless, I went along with his desire to quit, saying, "Yes, I do think it is an intolerable situation for you." I decided that for the moment he needed an ally. If I opposed him, he would quit anyway and would resent me and put me into the category of "enemy authority figure," which would cause him to quit therapy anyway. As it turned out, he quickly found another job and expressed appreciation that I had stood behind him. Hence, our therapeutic alliance was strengthened and we were able to get back to the basics of analysis.

Paradoxical

Lindner (1955) used joining effectively in working with a schizophrenic. The man had a delusion that he could travel to other planets and that he was the leader of a people on another planet. Instead of trying to tell the man he was delusional, Lindner decided to join the delusion. He began studying the patient's maps, helping him keep logs of his trips, and sending him back for more information. Eventually, the patient began to see the folly of it, and even to feel sorry for Lindner (whose delusion, he began to feel, was worse than his own).

The purpose of paradoxical joining is to highlight the absurdity of some kind of extreme but entrenched attitude, grandiosity, or delusion. All defensive postures are erected because people have felt opposed, attacked, demeaned, or sometimes annihilated in their childhoods. A child may be told, either verbally or nonverbally, that he will never amount to anything. He erects a defensive posture in which he imagines he is superior to everybody (especially his family). The family tries to make his attitude seem ridiculous, which it is; however, he persists in this grandiosity all the more. If you oppose such a defense, you will make it stronger. By joining it, you disarm it.

Paradoxical joining is sometimes necessary in order to break an impasse. Depressives and masochists may repeatedly attack themselves, saying, "I'm a loser, I'm hopeless, I'm a freak, I'm a goon. Why should anybody want to relate to me?" The normal, induced response of such statements is sympathy. The therapist wants to say, "You're fine. You're not hopeless." If you say that, you will be falling into a trap. The same trap the patient fell into when he or she tried to cheer up a depressed parent. Now, in the therapy office, that situation is being reversed, and the patient is being the depressed parent and is inducing the therapist to play the sympathetic and needy child.

To break the impasse, the therapist responds by joining the patient's attack on himself. "Yes, you're right. You are a loser. You are hopeless. You are a freak and a goon *right now.*" You are conveying that, at the moment, by attacking himself, he is enacting a self-fulfilling prophecy. At first the patient may think you're joking and say, "It's true, I'm a loser." However, if you persist in the joining, and are sincere, eventually the patient will begin to argue. "I'm not that much of a loser." And, incidentally, it's easy to be sincere, because after listening to the patient attack himself for several weeks or months you will begin to be convinced, as well as irritated. Showing this irritation is essential to the success of the intervention. Deep down, the patient knows he is annoying, and letting him know that you know he is annoying is helpful to him. It puts the relationship on a reality basis and establishes trust.

Traumatized patients also often require joining. When patients have just gone through some catastrophe they may be in a rage and will surely be in shock. Invariably, they feel like victims. You must join them in their need to feel like victims and to find scapegoats on whom to pin their rage, even though you may think they brought it on themselves. Sometimes that joining is straightforward, sometimes paradoxical. Hence, a young male patient who had an automobile accident on the day he was to be married was not wanting to hear that he had the accident to get out of the marriage. "Damn my luck," he cried. "I don't know why I'm always so unlucky! Why did that street have to be wet on that day? Why did my brakes have to stop working at that very moment? I'm just unlucky." I nodded and said, "It's rotten luck. It really is." But there was something a little too flip in my answer. He looked up and smiled wryly. "You think I did it on purpose, is that what you think?" I said nothing more. "Well, what if I did? I mean, she pressured me into this thing . . . ."

EXPRESSIVE TECHNIQUES

Under the category of expressive techniques I include emotional expression used by the therapist for dramatic effect, as well as facial gestures. I also include techniques from expressive therapies, that is, from art, dance, poetry, and music therapies.

Expressive techniques work well with hysterics, who tend themselves to be overdramatic, as well as with borderlines, schizophrenics, and manic-depressives (many of whom are artists). Often a grunt or facial expression can convey more than words ever could.

Straightforward

Having directed a cooperative therapy center in New York that specializes in therapy for people in the arts, I have had many occasions to use expressive techniques. Artists will often bring in their artworks. Like most therapists, I treat such works like dreams and try to interpret them. On occasion I will have a musician sing. Once, knowing that a particular patient had suffered much emotional pain at the time he was learning to play the trombone, I had him bring his instrument to my office and play it. In doing so he got in touch with a lot of sadness, and many new memories came to the surface. On other occasions I have had a patient sing a song that came into his mind during a session, and asked dancers to dance. For patients who are suicidal or in some crisis that is causing them to be bloated with anger, I have them act out their feelings, talk to the person they hate, and hit the couch with their fists. This often aids them in venting, which is necessary for them to move on.

Of course, using such expressive techniques is quite a departure from standard procedure. The patient is suddenly thrown into a different relationship with the therapist. She is suddenly dancing around his office, and he is looking on like an admiring parent. The patient may assume that the boundaries of the therapy have changed and be tempted to take more liberties. Hence it is important for the therapist to explain that he is departing from standard procedure and to convey through his tone and manner that although the therapy has become more active, the boundaries are still the same. It is important in any therapy experience for the patient to always feel a sense of safety and stability with regard to the boundaries; this protects him or her from the fear that either therapist or patient will lose control or give in to temptations.

Paradoxical

A young male artist had trouble figuring out whether or not his mother had loved him. Whenever I asked him if he had ever felt loved by his mother, he would say, "I'm not sure I know what love is. But she must have loved me. She always said she did." I had him draw a picture of his mother and told him, "Try to draw her as if she were the Mona Lisa. Have her looking at you in an ambiguous, mysterious way, so that you can't tell if she loves you or not." He laughed, but agreed to do it. However, no matter how hard he tried to make her eyes and her smile ambiguous (erasing the drawing again and again), the eyes always came out looking hard, and the smile always had a downward turn. "She hates me," he finally proclaimed.

A histrionic patient used to continually manufacture crises in her life in order to have reasons to vent feelings, thereby displacing them onto whoever was around her—including the therapist. Paradoxically, I had her think of all the people and situations in her life that were giving her fits. When she had finished I asked her to think of more, and then more. Meanwhile I had her pummel the couch with her fists harder and harder and to tell them all off. "Come on, you can do better than that," I kept saying. "I want to see a *real* fit." When she realized that her fit was not accomplishing the purpose she hoped for (getting me agitated and angry at her), she stopped hitting and screaming and began to cry like a little girl. After a while she mumbled, "No one ever took me seriously."

USING COUNTERTRANSFERENCE FEELINGS TO DETERMINE TECHNIQUE

Integrating eclectic techniques into a psychoanalytic framework is not so easy. As a beginning therapist—filled with my own kind of I-can-do-anything narcissism—I used to think it was easy. I would blithely command my patients to do this and to do that and sometimes I would get spectacular results (sort of like those fundamentalist ministers who perform faith healing and other miracles in front of an awed congregation). I soon realized that those results were due to the informal hypnotic induction that had thrown my patients into infantilized transference states. As long as they were in these states and for some time afterward they seemed improved. Some symptoms would never return. However, eventually they would shift into negative transferences and their basic characterology would resume causing the same problems in their careers and relationships as before. I had to come to grips with the fact that the spectacular and sensational in therapy (as in life) had almost nothing to do with the truth. In reality, therapy is almost invariably a subtle, grind-it-out, long-term procedure.

Learning to use eclectic techniques in a grounded way took years of training, supervision, and experience. However, if there is a key to using such techniques, it is surely self-understanding. The single most important job that any therapist has to do is to be able to analyze his or her own countertransference. Therapists must always analyze their own transference and resistance before analyzing the transferences and resistances of their patients (Schoenewolf 1993). To do otherwise is to put the cart before the horse. Moreover, the single most important distinction therapists must make is whether the feelings and thoughts they are having about each patient are being induced by that patient or are coming from their own subjective countertransference.

This is a difficult distinction to make, for the capacity of all human beings—including therapists—to deceive themselves is infinite. Our own narcissism causes us to want to think that we are beyond having subjective countertransference reactions, that we have already done our therapy, for God's sake, and therefore the feelings must have been induced by the patient. Unfortunately, there is no way for a therapist to be sure of this distinction. Only the kind of self-awareness that comes from years of supervision and training can help to guarantee that such a distinction is a valid one.

There are usually clues to help us know when the feelings we are having toward a patient are coming from our own unresolved past business. If there is some edge to our feelings, some undertow of anxiety, that is usually a sign that they are not truly grounded and objective. For example, a patient continually comes late and we become annoyed. We interpret her lateness, as we should, but for some unexplainable reason we are angry when we do so, and we hear our voice getting a bit husky. A therapist must be diligent in paying attention to the quality of his or her responses to a patient, looking out for a spurt of inexplicable emotion that might creep out, a stubbornness that is not appropriate, or an anxious what-have-I-done-now feeling at the pit of one's stomach after one has made what one thought was a proper response.

Once we are able to make these distinctions, we can use our countertransference feelings to help determine what technique to use with a particular patient and when and how to use it. A patient mumbles through session after session, stopping and starting, stuttering through words. I find myself getting angry at her, wanting to yell, "Speak up." I study the feelings and recognize they are being induced. Her father had been dominating and intrusive; he used to hit her on the head if she did not remember the multiplication tables precisely. Now she is inducing me and others in her life to hit her on the head. Unwittingly, she wants to transfer onto me the quality of relating she had in the past. I use this information to decide on an intervention. I give her an emotional communication with a constructive rather than destructive tilt. "You know," I tell her, "I've been finding myself feeling annoyed by you, wanting to yell at you, wanting to hit you on the head, and I realize that it's because I feel frustrated by the way you keep mumbling and stuttering and stopping and starting. I'm really interested in hearing what you have to say, and I'd really like to hear it. Then I remembered what you told me about your father, how he used to hit you on the head every time you couldn't recite the multiplication tables and I felt sympathy for you. It would be helpful to me and to the therapeutic process if you could speak up a bit." After repeating this again and again, the patient's stuttering gradually began to diminish.

In another case I found myself wanting to go to sleep whenever a middle-aged male patient was in my office. This was in the beginning stages of therapy, and he refused to lie on the couch. He had a need to keep me under surveillance, so his dark, beady eyes were always upon me. At the same time, he spoke in a low, unemotional, monotonous voice. The combination of being constantly probed with his eyes and lulled by his voice put me to sleep. Underneath my drowsiness were feelings he was inducing in me. He was totally denying the rage he was feeling and projecting it onto me. Therefore, he had to constantly probe me to be ready for any rage that might emerge from me and threaten to get out of control. Being so treated, I found myself getting enraged. However, like him, I quickly suppressed it. That took up a lot of energy and made me tired. So my eyes would begin blinking. Then I would be afraid he would see me blinking and that would make me blink even more.

I thought about all this and was able to understand it and devise an eclectic intervention. I began to blink spasmodically, hoping he would notice. Surprisingly, he never said anything about it. It was I who had to bring it up. "I find myself blinking a lot. Have you noticed?"

"Yes. Is something the matter?"

"Something is making me tired. Something is making me want to go to sleep." I didn't say that "he" was making me go to sleep. That would have been too threatening.

"What is it that's making you go to sleep?"

"That's what I want to find out."

I treated the whole think like a mystery that I needed his help to investigate. It was a kind of behavioral technique, a research assignment for us to pursue together. Instead of threatening him, it aroused his curiosity. "Maybe it's the time of day?" he asked. It was midafternoon. I said, "No, that's not it." "Maybe it's too hot in here." "No, I don't feel hot." Finally he said, "Maybe it's me." I asked what he meant. "Well, I find that people in my life are always turning away from me. I mean, when I'm on the subway, I look at people and they quickly look away, like I have some kind of disease. Maybe it's the way I look at people. My wife says I stare and make people uncomfortable." The ensuing discussion came back to our relationship and his feelings about me, and was quite fruitful in exploring resistance, transference, and ego-functioning.

If therapists pay attention to the feelings that are being induced by patients (and they are being induced moment by moment) they will get a fix on where the patient is, developmentally and transferentially. These feelings, in combination with the therapist's training and experience, will enable them to understand how to respond. Often, you become the container for feelings or memories that the patient does not want to own. If you are feeling anxious, probably the patient is disowning and projecting anxiety; if you are feeling angry, he is disowning and projecting anger; if you are feeling sexually aroused, often he is disowning and projecting his erotic feelings. Often such feelings were disowned and projected in his family.

In the teaching tales that follow, I have tried to show not only how I used eclectic psychodynamic therapy, but also how my understanding of my own feelings helped me to do so.

PART II

TEACHING
TALES

CHAPTER 2

Buttons

Directive Questioning in a Case of Sexual Molestation

"I hate them," she said matter-of-factly. She lay quite still and spoke in a soft, thoughtful voice. "I don't know why but they make me sick. They make me want to faint. If I see one on a table, for instance, or on a man's shirt, I want to throw up or faint. I can't stand seeing them. I can't stand thinking about them."

"Do you feel sick now?"

"Yes."

"You don't sound sick."

"That's because I'm detached. I'm usually detached. I've always been detached. I don't know why. But at the same time, in some wretched recess deep inside me, I feel sick."

"Do you only get sick when you see them on a man's shirt, or do you also get sick when you see them on a woman's blouse or dress?"

"Men's shirts are worse."

"Is it only the plastic ones that make you sick? Suppose they're made of leather or brass or ivory?"

"No, just the plastic ones."

"What is it about plastic?"

"I don't know. I've never been able to figure it out. I wish I could understand it. I've tried to understand it all my life. I'm just obsessed with them. I've always been obsessed with them.''

The subject was buttons. Plastic buttons. The kind found on men's shirts, pants, or suits. The woman exploring this subject lay on the couch in front of me, her arms at her sides, the palms pressed against the mattress like suction cups. She was a thin, pale, thirtyish woman, with eyes dimmed by medication that had been prescribed for her epilepsy, yet eyes that still leaked occasional tiny glints of anxiety and rage as she spoke. From her earliest teens she had been given the message by her parents and by their doctors that she was defective and that her epilepsy as well as countless other symptoms were due to this defectiveness. This attitude was maintained despite the fact that at one point during her adolescence, following an epileptic seizure, she was admitted to a mental hospital where she was diagnosed as schizotypal, with epileptic and anorexic features. She was told that her condition was strictly organic and that nothing could be done about it except taking medication to maintain her convulsions and her eating disorder.

During our first session, she told me I was her first therapist. She had been afraid to go to a therapist before, afraid to contradict her parents and their doctors, who had been so adamant that her condition was organic. It was as though contradicting them would be a deep insult to their pride, would in fact injure them in some huge way. However, by the end of this first session she said that she thought something really good was going to come out of the therapy. After the second, she said she felt really safe in my office. During the third she started talking about buttons. Now, in our fourth, she had plunged into the well of her repression.

"Priscilla, have you always been obsessed with buttons?" I persisted. I assumed that the buttons were most likely a screen memory, covering up another deeper and more traumatic memory.

"Always."

"Plastic buttons?"

"Yes. I can't stand them. I have to look away whenever I see one. I try not to look at people's clothes, because of the buttons. I always keep my eyes on their faces or their hands. If I glance at a button, I'll start thinking about it and won't be able to stop until I get myself sick."

"Why do they make you sick?"

"Because they're repulsive."

"What's repulsive about them?"

She shook her head. "I don't like to talk about it."

"Are they *that* repulsive?"

"Yes. I can't explain it. I hate them. I hate the small ones and the big ones. I hate the white ones and the black ones. They just repulse me. I wish I could understand it. I wish I wasn't obsessed."

"What comes to mind when you think of buttons?"

"What comes to mind?"

"Do any memories come to mind?"

"For some reason I just remembered the time I got molested. I don't know what this has to do with anything." She turned half around toward me. "I was hiking up a mountain with four other girls. I don't know why I'm thinking about this. It has nothing to do with buttons."

"Go on."

"I haven't thought about this in a long time, in years. I used to have nightmares about it." She lay as if at attention, her arms at her sides, her legs slightly apart, gazing at the bookcases at the foot of the couch. From her stillness I knew that she had become cataleptic and had gone into a trance. I could see her eyes behind her steel-rimmed glasses, pale blue, sky blue, perhaps the color of the sky the day she took her hike, eyes that were in retreat from that hike and its aftermath, in flight from earth and its turnings. Outside my window the sky was also blue, and you could hear the cars buzzing by, but this sky of today was a bustling sky far removed from the nightmare sky of her childhood.

"I've never talked about this to anybody since it happened. It's all very vague. I think there were five of us, five girls. We were hiking up the mountain in the order of our height, the tallest girl first and so on. I was the shortest." She chuckled with surprise and bitterness. "I was always the shortest. So I was last."

"How old were you then?"

"I'm not sure. I think I was about 7. I was in the first or second grade. Something like that."

"And you were hiking up the mountain by yourselves."

"Yes. Actually, it wasn't really a mountain, more like a hill, a little wooded hill on a large empty lot near my house. So there we were, five little girls walking up the hill, and then we ran into this man. I don't remember what he looked like. I think he was pretty old, but I'm not sure. I think he approached us and offered each of us a penny to take off our clothes. He went up to each girl. Since I was the shortest, he came up to me last. I knew I was going to have to say yes."

"Why did you have to say yes?"

"Because they all said no, and somebody had to say yes."

"Why did somebody have to say yes?"

"Because I didn't want to hurt his feelings. I had been taught that you had to please adults."

"Who taught you that?"

"My parents. I could never say no to them. I could never say no to my mother because she'd fall apart if I did."

"What do you mean, fall apart?"

"She'd get very quiet and this look—this look of betrayal—would scrunch up her face like a prune and she wouldn't talk to me or anybody for days. Maybe a few days later she'd say something to my father and then he'd yell at me."

"And you couldn't say no to your father either?"

"No. But he was a little better than my mother."

"He was a little better?"

"If I said no to him he'd get angry, but he wouldn't fall apart like my mother."

"But you didn't want to hurt his feelings."

"No. I didn't want to hurt his feelings or my mother's. I had to be good."

"And you didn't want to hurt the man's feelings. The molester on the hill."

"Right. I had to say yes. I just had to, don't you see that?"

"Yes, I see. Then what happened?"

"He gave me a penny and I took off my clothes. I think he gave me a penny. Everything's vague at this point. I know I pulled down my pants. I don't remember what he looked like. I was so short I could only see his crotch. I could—" Her eyes opened wide. "Oh, God." She sat up and pulled her knees against herself. "I'm getting that feeling of disgust, the same feeling I have when I see buttons." She rocked forward and back, quickly, urgently, then looked back at me in terror. "I don't want to remember this." She slid to the edge of the couch, away from me, and shook her head, gazing across the room. "Oh, God, I think I'm going to be sick."

I felt an impulse to hug her or shake her. I did nothing of the kind, of course, for I had discovered that it is when therapists act out the feelings that patients induce in them that they most often get into trouble. Instead I tried to understand why she was inducing these feelings in me. I recalled Freud's case of the Rat Man. The Rat Man, having been terrorized by his father, had often jumped up from the couch during his sessions with Freud, assuming that Freud was going to beat him as his father had. Perhaps she had a conflicting desire to be slapped or hugged by me, rooted in the primal feelings of terror she herself experienced.

Priscilla had never been beaten, but her boundaries had never been respected. She had told me in previous sessions that when she had become an adolescent and had grown her first pubic hairs, she had rushed to her mother in horror and her mother had taken her into the bathroom and cut them with a scissors. When she got her first period her mother bought her a box of sanitary napkins and took charge of inserting them and removing them. Thereafter, each month her mother continued to be preoccupied with her period. At the same time she repeatedly warned her and her older sister not to act like sluts. She continually monitored the way they dressed and the expressions on their faces or bodies, checking for sluttiness. The older sister rebelled against this monitoring by becoming wild and willful. Priscilla took the alternate route, becoming, as she put it, "a goody two-shoes." Her father teased her mercilessly about her budding breasts, her periods, her infatuations. Meanwhile, her grandfather, who lived with them, would walk into the bathroom while she was sitting on the toilet or bathing and sometimes stroll up to her, beam good-naturedly, and tickle her crotch.

The result of all this disrespect of her boundaries was to prevent her from separating from her parents and establishing her own real self, with her own feelings and thoughts and values. It kept her sexually and assertively repressed and stuffed up with an accumulation of frustration, which in turn created a masochistic orientation, the masochism that had been such a crucial characterological factor in her having been the girl who was molested. Wilhelm Reich (1933) noted that severe, traumatic punishments of infantile sexuality is often related to a masochistic character development. Shirley Panken (1975) observed that fathers of masochists are "angry, critical, or undermining" while "markedly inadequate and threatened by the mother," and that mothers of masochists are "phallic, seductive, overwhelming, or castrating," and tend to be martyrs who are "contemptuous of their husbands and rejecting of their feminine role" (p. 91). These statements seemed to fit Priscilla's case almost exactly.

I thought of these and related things and then asked, "Are you feeling frightened now?"

"I don't know." She was huddled at the foot of the couch, crouched over, hugging herself. "Yes, maybe that's it. I feel scared. That must be it. I didn't realize I was feeling scared."

"You didn't know you were feeling scared?"

"No. I never know what I'm feeling."

"What are you scared of?"

She looked up at the bookcase before her.

"Of the bookcase?"

"No."

"Of the room?"

"No."

"Of me?"

She looked around. "I never thought of that." She seemed to be relieved as soon as she thought of it. "Maybe that's it. I don't know why I'd be scared of you." She lay back down on her side, turned toward the room, resting her chin on her hand. "I often feel scared when I'm alone with a man."

"You're alone with a man now."

"Yes."

She lay down again with her hands at her sides and the palms turned downward.

"What scares you about being alone with a man?"

"I guess I'm afraid you'll do something . . . sexual."

"Have I behaved in a way that makes you think I'm going to be sexual?"

"No. But you might anyway. I just think all men are going to be sexual. Like my grandfather. Like the man on the hill." She gazed across the room at a patch of light that shone from the window. I kept as still as possible. I was afraid that one squeak of my chair would send her out of the room. Her voice became trancelike again. "I can't remember what happened exactly. Everything's so vague. I think . . . I think he touched me. I think . . . oh, God . . . no . . . I think he had sex with me." She made this exclamation without a change in her voice. "I actually think he had sex with me. He must have, but I was only a little girl. How could he? I was so small." She was depersonalizing, witnessing the scene as though it were happening to somebody else. All of a sudden real feelings broke to the surface and a small sob spurted out and a look of shock overtook her face. She quickly caught the sob in her throat and suppressed it and her voice became flat again. "I don't know what happened to the other girls," she said, as though merely curious. "I think they had gone down the hill. No, they were standing to one side. I wish I hadn't said yes. I feel guilty that I was the only one to say yes." She sighed but remained still. Her eyes were looking fixedly at the crack of light across the room. "I can remember what he was wearing. He was wearing . . . yes, now I remember . . . he was wearing long underwear, the kind with buttons all over the crotch and up the behind. He was wearing long underwear, and it took him a while to undo the buttons." She was looking across the room, and her eyes flickered as she gazed at the revisualized scene.

"What kind of buttons were they?"

"White, plastic buttons. Large ones. I'm feeling faint just thinking about them. Maybe I shouldn't talk about this. Should I talk about this?"

"It's up to you. I think it would be good if you could."

"I . . . I think . . . I'm trying to remember what happened next. . . . I think he only touched me with his fingers. . . . Oh, God, I don't want to think he had sex with me. But I think he did. Or maybe he touched me with his penis.'' A look of terror rippled across her face and another spurt of sobbing came out. She rolled over on her side, facing the wall, and sobbed just a moment, then caught herself and lay back again. There was a new determination in her eyes. ''I saw . . . his penis,'' she said, shaking her head.

''You saw it?''

''Yes. I was repulsed. Come to think of it, I feel the same way about penises as I do about buttons. They repulse me. I haven't had sex with my boyfriend in a year. I was repulsed about the whole thing, about everything to do with sex.'' A brief aftersob leapt from her mouth and she gazed at the patch of light and pleaded, ''I didn't want to say yes. All the other girls had said no, so I knew when it was my turn I was going to have to say yes. I had to, you see? Afterward he gave each girl a penny. But when he came to me, he didn't have a penny. He had a button in his hand, just like the buttons on his long underwear, and he gave me the button, smiling as though he were giving me a piece of gold. 'You only got a button,' one of the girls said to me later as we walked down the hill. I felt disappointed that I only got a button, after I was the one who had said yes.''

''Did they find the man?''

''When I got home I tried to tell my mother what happened, but she didn't want to hear it. She kept saying, 'That's all right, it's over now,' and she called the police. When the police came I couldn't remember anything. I couldn't even remember what his face looked like. I had only looked at his crotch. Another girl remembered his face. The police and the fire department went up onto the hill looking for him, but they never found him. Afterward my mother took me out for an ice cream cone. 'You deserve a treat,' she said, 'after what you've gone through.' It was the biggest ice cream cone I ever had. It was huge. Mom was always like that, using food to stuff down feelings. Dad too. My whole family was like that, going back generations.''

"So you never got a chance to talk to anybody about this?''

"No, never. Like I said, Mom couldn't stand ever to hear me suffer. She couldn't stand any negative feelings. So I had to keep everything in. I was a good little girl.''

"Never expressed any anger, any fear, any rage?''

"Never. I never let out a squawk, until I was 15.''

"What happened then?''

"That's when I had my first grand mal. We were sitting at the kitchen table talking about food or something. We were always talking about food. Always about food, never about feelings. We were talking about cereal or some such thing, my parents and me, and I felt myself begin to twitch, and then my head shot around as though pulled by some kind of dark force, and I started screaming, and I fell to the floor and passed out. Mom took me to a doctor who diagnosed epilepsy, and he prescribed medication.''

"Did anybody ever ask what you were feeling, what made you scream?''

"No. Never.''

She let out another terrified sob, and as she did I could feel the terrified little girl that had been so long locked inside Priscilla, who had now at last broken out, and I could imagine in my mind's eye how she had said yes to the molester, assuming it was her responsibility to say yes to him, just as it had been her responsibility to say yes to her parents in contradistinction to her older sister's constant no. She had never been taught she had the right to say no, to have her own self, to harbor her own views, or even her own feelings; her job was to smile and say yes and take care of her parents' feelings. Her duty was to accede to her grandfather's pawing. Her mission was to be the good girl they all wanted, the good patsy.

I saw in my mind's eye the terrified little girl as she stood before the molester, and I also saw an angry little girl, who perceived in this incident an opportunity to unleash some of her frustration by giving in to this molester, giving in out of spite, being for that instant the slut her mother had warned her not to be. For she had been given double messages by her family: on the one hand, she was to do everything they (and other adults) asked of her and to deny them nothing, and on the other hand, she was to say no to being a slut. Her mother was telling her not to be a slut, but her grandfather was pawing her. Now this man was asking her to do something, yet he was also asking her to be a slut. She could not say no, and she could not say yes. What should she do? I could imagine the scene as if it were being played out in that instant, see the little girl pulling down her pants, her eyes at the level of the molester's long underwear as he unbuttoned the crotch. See his ordinary face. See the other girls standing to one side in shock. Did the man actually have sex with her? It's hard to say. He may have touched her with his hand and in her hysterical memory of it she imagined that he had had sex with her. Or he may have touched her with his penis. Or he may have penetrated her. But if he had penetrated her, would she not have bled? I could see the blood, and then I could see no blood and just her eyes stunned as she gazed at the buttons of his underwear and his hand played around as he masturbated himself.

I could see the homecoming drama, see her mother's hasty attempt to avoid dealing with the incident, her swift dangling of an ice cream cone at her daughter's mouth to keep her from uttering bad words. Did the mother wonder how the girl was feeling? Did she check to see if she was bleeding? Apparently not. Perhaps the mother was enraged, enraged that her daughter had committed this slutty behavior in spite of her repeated warnings. I could imagine the rantings and ravings by this mother both before and after this incident, the warnings against sluthood that were in fact dares (as such warnings inevitably are), which challenged her daughters to be either feverishly anti- or pro-slut. I could see a mother who was so obsessed with her daughter's sexuality that she had created self-defeating attitude about sexuality, one that culminated in that molestation on the hill.

I could see the father lying back in his chair watching television, a fat, hostile man who added insult to injury in this dysfunctional family system by aggressing against his already-deflated daughter. I imagined a man whose eyes and cheeks were red and puffy from eating and watching television, who would turn to his daughter only to laugh at or taunt her. He was a man who was extremely forbearing with adult women, but mean to his kids, a man who had himself been frustrated and blocked as a child. Then there was the grandfather, the father's father, who thought he was indulging in a little harmless grandfatherly affection in the bathroom, his eyes twinkling as his fingers grazed her body.

It was no wonder that her anger could only come out in starts and fits. The early psychoanalysts were on the right track, contending that not all epileptic fits were organic. "For purposes of discharge the instinct of destruction is habitually brought into the service of Eros," Freud (1928) wrote. "We suspect that the epileptic fit is a product and indication of an instinctual diffusion" (p. 229). Otto Fenichel (1945) noted the "very intense destructive and sadistic drives which have been repressed for a long time and which find an explosive discharge in the seizure" (p. 265). The grand mal seizure was the only outlet left for her to express her accumulated rage, and it was perfect disguise because it was so easily dismissed as some kind of sudden sickness that had nothing to do with her parents, nothing to do with their cruelty to her. And she went along with it, and the charade played itself out from doctor to doctor, medicine to medicine, and year to year.

I saw these things in that instant and suddenly detested her parents, no longer seeing them as human beings at all but as demons. For that moment I lost sight of objectivity and identified completely with the repressed little girl that had now hatched in the pale afternoon light of my office. I wanted to rail at the parents or soothe Priscilla and tell her nobody would ever abuse her again. However, as she sobbed once, twice, then three times, before falling silent and somber again, I came back to myself and knew how wrong it would have been to have made a big deal out of her abuse, especially her sexual abuse. I had come to the recognition by then that although sexual abuse was harmful, it was no more harmful than the thousands of much subtler types of verbal and emotional abuse that can happen in dysfunctional family systems and are so hard to detect—the double binds and scapegoating and triangling that can so confuse the developing ego and derail the normal will to mastery. I had long ceased to be involved in the politicizing of sexual abuse, or in the trend toward viewing it as a men-against-women thing. It was just what it was: another form of blighted emotional development, no more and no less. The molestation on the hill was important, but it could not have had nearly the effect it had if it were not for the seeds that were planted in the dysfunctional family environment, and the response to the molestation and to her fits.

Had I made a big deal out of her sexual abuse, I would have become overinvolved with her just as her mother had done; hence, I would have unwittingly replicated the faulty rearing of her childhood. No, I would not and could not be a fellow sobber, an ax grinder, or avenging angel. I would not and could not be an empathic co-victim nor an overprotective parent. I could not be a "sister" who joined her anger against men. What I could be, though, was what I was, a man and a therapist. I could simply be there without ado and hope that she might discover on her own that a man could have empathy for her and not exploit her sexually, and to experience the kind of strength that had been lacking from her own father, who withdrew into his syndrome of eating and watching television and hurling displaced taunts at her.

"So you never talked about the sexual abuse with anybody?" I asked again after a while. She lay hugging herself, her thin, pale arms curled around her as if made of clay, as if they could be stretched and snapped like clay. Her equally thin legs were crossed at the knees and her brows were furrowed. "You never mentioned it at all?"

"No. I never even thought about it until now."

"And then when you were 15 you had your first epileptic seizure."

"Yes."

"What happened when you were 15?"

"My sister left home. She went away to college."

"And that upset you?"

"Yes. I don't know why. While she was there, as long as she was still living in the house, still a part of the family, I was okay. But after she left, I had to put up with both my mother and father. I had to deal with them by myself. I guess my sister, in her way, had been some kind of buffer. She had always been the rebel, and they had concentrated a lot of their energy on her. When she left, I became the target. There was nobody there but me. Nobody. Oh, God. I never realized how upset I was at that time. I was so upset, so confused. . . ."

She continued to talk in a thoughtful, almost languorous voice. The terror had left her and she was calm and centered. I sat back and let her talk, let her discover. I was suddenly aware again of the New York traffic and the blue of the sky. We had gone on a little trip together and now we had returned and the city was still there and the sky was still blue, but a paler blue, as if to acknowledge a loss, or perhaps to soothe it.

CHAPTER 3

Beginnings and Endings

Expressive and Mirroring Techniques to Head Off Abortive Beginnings and Premature Endings

Beginnings and endings are the most crucial times for all relationships, including therapeutic ones. This does not mean that the events between beginnings and endings are not important, but they do not have the same urgency.

How a mother begins her relationship with her infant sets the tone for everything that is to come. How a therapist begins the therapeutic relationship with a patient also sets the tone for everything that is to come. If a mother is too sadistic or masochistic, she will likely raise masochistic or sadistic children; if she is too depressed, she will likely raise depressed children; if she is happy and loving, she will likely raise happy and loving children.

Likewise, if therapists are sadistic or masochistic with patients, their patients will probably react sadistically or masochistically. If they are depressed, their patients will most likely become resentful, anxious, pitying, or depressed themselves. If they are happy and loving, their patients will grow. And by a happy and loving therapist I mean one who behaves in such a way as to nurture the patient. Nurturing a patient may at times require listening, at times talking, at times getting angry, at times apologizing, at times nodding even though you do not agree, at times drawing the line. The nurturing process starts from the onset, and what it requires is that the therapist be in perfect tune with the patient, ready to respond in whatever way is required by the situation.

A BEGINNING

Many a therapy relationship is botched from the beginning because the therapist is not prepared to be spontaneous. Above all, an eclectic psychoanalytic approach requires spontaneity and a readiness to deal with whatever a patient brings in. One of my more extreme beginnings comes to mind.

A difficult type to deal with, especially in the beginning, is the angry borderline or paranoid patient. Usually these types will come to the first session ready to test you to the limits. They will try to rile you and then knock you down in order to prove that you are not worthy of them. This will allow them to maintain their defensive posture of suspicion and retain their delusions of superiority.

A young man of this kind, whom I will call Mr. N. (for nod), about whom I have previously written (Schoenewolf 1993), came to the consultation with an angry scowl on his face. He sat down in the chair I assigned him without taking his eyes off of me. After a rather long silence, during which he scrutinized everything about me and my office with obvious disdain, he began to interrogate me.

"What are your qualifications?" he asked in a cold, suspicious tone of voice.

I replied calmly and without, I hoped, any malice, nervousness, or sweetness, though it did not make me feel good to be questioned in such a hostile and superior way. "I have a Ph.D. in psychology. I've graduated from a psychoanalytic institute. I'm a certified psychoanalyst."

"Where did you get your Ph.D.?"

Again, I answered calmly. Even though his manner was hostile, and he was demanding information that I did not think it necessary for him to know, I went along with him. "My diplomas are there on the wall," I said.

He stood up to study the wall of diplomas. He must have looked at each one for several minutes. At least that is how long it felt to me.

"What kind of technique do you use?" he asked, sitting down.

"I'm eclectic. I use whatever works."

"That sounds too broad. Aren't you a psychoanalyst?"

"Yes."

"Then how can you be eclectic?"

"I'm an eclectic psychoanalyst."

"That sounds like a malapropism."

"Does it?"

"How can a psychoanalyst be eclectic? Either you're a psychoanalyst or your another kind of therapist."

"Why can't I be a psychoanalyst who uses other methods as well?"

"It sounds suspicious."

He fired more questions like a defense attorney trying to break a witness. I kept answering calmly. I was biding my time. I knew from the moment he had walked in that he was going to try to knock me down, and I knew that I was going to have to counter him in some way. I was not sure yet how I was going to do it. I was like a boxer who is taking a lot of hits in order to study the style of his opponent; I had to let him take a few punches before I would know how and when to make my own move.

About ten or fifteen minutes later, after he had begun reluctantly and sulkily to give me a few bits and pieces of his life history, always keeping me under strict surveillance with his probing brown eyes, the moment of truth came. He had this stop-and-start manner and questioning tone in his voice. He would say something in his stumbling manner, then stop and stare at me, as if to say, "Well, are you listening?" This caused me to nod somewhat emphatically. Then he would say something else, look up, and I would nod again.

Suddenly he said, "Do you always nod like an idiot?"

My first reaction was to feel stunned. Then I was furious. There were about two or three seconds of silence before I replied. In those seconds I regained my composure and understood that he was inducing in me an urge to kick him out of my office. I speculated that he probably induced that feeling in others, and that in his childhood he had been enraged to the point of either wanting to kick somebody, or wanting to be kicked, out of the house. I also knew that this was the moment I was waiting for. He had made what I thought was his major attack, and this was where I needed to make my counterattack.

In a flash I realized that he would require a paradoxical technique to prod him out of his defensive posture. I looked at him, smiled very brightly, and nodded my head several times exaggeratedly, while at the same time emitting a noise such as a donkey might make: "Yeeuk! Yeeuk! Yeeuk!" Then I stopped smiling and just looked at him. It was sort of a Zen moment (Fromm et al. 1960).

Now it was his turn to be stunned. The scowl left his face and his dark probing eyes dropped down to the floor. He was silent for a moment, then he continued talking, more earnestly now, about his history. He no longer probed me with his eyes as he talked, but kept them down. It was clear that I had passed the test and that he was now ready to take me into his confidence. Neither he nor I said anything about the idiotic noise. It had come and gone like the blink of an eye, yet it was of crucial significance.

Had I tried to use a verbal reply to his attack, it would

not have worked. If I had tried a standard psychoanalytic approach, such as an interpretation, "You appear to see me as a ridiculous figure who is pretending to listen to you but is really not," I am certain he would have pounced on such a statement. Had I retorted, "Yes, that's right, sometimes I do nod a lot. What does that mean to you?" he would have been equally ready to bash me. I was convinced, based on past experiences with such types, that he would not have trusted any kind of technique. What people with his particular disturbance usually trust, and what he *did* trust, was an honest human nonverbal communication.

Through that interchange I had told him, nonverbally, that I accepted myself, accepted that I could be quite idiotic, and that I could tolerate his aggression. It was important for him to know that, in order for him to depend on me. I also told him that I did not hold his aggression against him. I was not hostile—my intent being not to hurt him, but to indicate that I understood what he was doing, understood the depths of his rage, and that it had annoyed but not hurt me. Had I shown hostility rather than a simple reactive gesture—had I said, "Do *you* always talk like an idiot?"—he might have felt victorious in that he had succeeded in provoking me to counterattack in a nasty way, engaging me in his displaced power struggle. In that case he would most likely have made a hasty retreat, getting in one last dig on his way out: "Thanks for your time, Doc."

As it turned out, Mr. N. did sign on for therapy. Several sessions later he brought up the nodding incident, referring to my "defensiveness" on that occasion. I asked what he meant by my defensiveness. He said he thought I had acted defensive when he had made an observation about my nodding too much. He did not recall that he had said I nodded "like an idiot." I had to remind him of that. (It is

almost universal to want to deny our own aggression.)
Anyway, we were able to discuss the episode and, by
doing so, begin the analysis of resistance and transference
and start the working-through process.

AN ENDING

Endings may be even more difficult to handle than beginnings, and in therapy they are always meaningful. Most of
the time, patients want to end the relationship prematurely. Indeed, most of the time they want to end the
relationship just at the point when the negative transference rears its ugly head. They have gone along doing what
they usually do in the beginning of relationships—
showing their good side, appeasing, trying to impress,
trying to entertain, enjoying being listened to, feeling
exhilarated by a new experience of intimacy. Then the
honeymoon is over. Something usually happens to end it,
anything from a casual gesture or remark by the therapist
to his summer vacation. Suddenly patients begin to have
fears of being too dependent, of being controlled or
manipulated, of being devalued, of being sexually or
financially exploited or abused, of being abandoned, of
going crazy, of driving the therapist crazy, of having some
violent and earth-shattering confrontation, and numerous
other outcomes.

But, naturally, they do not tell you any of this, nor are
they themselves necessarily in touch with it. What they
generally tell you is, "I've decided to stop therapy for a
while." They think if they say "for a while" it will soften
the blow and demonstrate that they really are committed.
"I just can't afford it anymore," they say. "I lost my

job . . . didn't get the promotion I wanted . . . too much child-support . . . I have other priorities." Then they invariably go on to say, "It's not resistance. Believe me. I know you're going to say that. But it's not. I really like therapy. You've helped me so much. I really appreciate all you've done for me. It's just the money. That's all it is. Really. I wish you'd believe me for once."

The usual response to this typical way of ending therapy is anger. You want to say, "Fine. Good-bye." You fantasize about going to the door, opening it, and pointing your thumb indecently toward the exit sign. You realize they're acting out their feelings by leaving therapy in this way, and that they fancy themselves to be quite clever. They have dismissed you without admitting that they are dismissing you, devalued you without acknowledging that they are devaluing you, blown you away while smilingly avowing how much they appreciate you.

And yet, if you can keep your head at such times, you can turn the occasion to your—and the patient's—advantage. For it is just at such times that the very biggest leaps can occur and the most can be learned by the patient.

Several techniques are helpful for such occasions. In some instances, with patients who are too narcissistic or paranoid to accept anything but a straightforward joining technique, I will simply say, "You know what's best. I wish you well." This sometimes throws them. They may then say, "I expected you to try to talk me into staying." This leads to an exploration of their projections. "I felt you were just trying to financially exploit me." Sometimes the matter is resolved at that point. Others actually do leave; if so it may be that they are simply not yet ready to go further, no matter what. Certain patients must repeat the cycle of starting and stopping therapy a number of times before they're ready to settle down with one therapist, perhaps indicative of a fixation at the "practicing"

stage of development (Mahler et al. 1975), the stage at
which a toddler practices walking away and returning to
Mother. Some return to therapy later knowing that they
can stop whenever they want.

On other occasions, if the patient is wavering, I will use
a different approach. One of my recent patients was of this
variety. I could tell that Mr. Q. (for quit), a man in his early
30s, was not absolutely sure about quitting, and I knew
that we had established a tenuous therapeutic alliance.
When he told me that he was quitting, I listened calmly.
He stated the usual reasons, having to do with not earning
enough money and, in his case, being "tired of therapy."
Almost invariably, after they have said they are quitting
and have given the reasons, patients will turn to me and
ask, "So what do you think?"

I usually reply, "I don't think it matters what I think."

"Why?" Mr. Q. asked.

"Well, if you had wanted to know what I thought, you
would have asked me before you made your decision to
leave."

"You're probably right. But I really do want to know
what you think. I might change my mind."

"I'll make a deal with you. I'll tell you what I think, but
only on one condition. The condition is that you put off
your decision to quit and continue for a few more sessions."

"Why should I continue for a few more sessions?"

"So that I can tell you what I think."

"It's going to take you that long to tell me what you
think?"

"That's right. And for us to bat it around."

"I don't know."

"What have you got to lose? What's your hurry to leave
therapy?"

"Nothing I guess."

Oftentimes this technique works. They continue and the urgency to leave evaporates. They begin to talk about what they are really feeling and the therapy moves forward.

Mr. Q. dutifully agreed to keep coming to therapy for a few more sessions, but I soon realized that he had done so only to defeat me. For three sessions I tried to work on him. I told him that people always wanted to leave therapy at a point when feelings and conflicts were coming to the surface that could not be tolerated. I said if he left therapy now, he would miss out on the opportunity to work through and learn from these feelings and resolve these conflicts. I told him he was acting out feelings he was having about me, and I urged him to tell me any negative thoughts he was having. He seemed to listen and even agreed with what I was saying.

But after the three sessions, he smiled tiredly and a bit pityingly, and said, "I'm sorry, but you haven't changed my mind. It's not you. The therapy has really helped me, and I understand what you're saying about missing out on an opportunity. But I really don't have any negative feelings about you or about therapy. It's mainly just the money, really. Why won't you just believe me?" He raised his brows and shrugged as if to say, "Sorry I can't help you out."

I pondered the situation in silence for a moment. I knew without any doubt that it would be wrong for him to leave. He had a repeating pattern of going enthusiastically into new relationships, then becoming disillusioned, then leaving. He had done that now with me. He started out enthusiastically and then seemed to settle in as a good patient. However, I knew he was holding back his negative feelings for me. Only on rare occasions would his contempt leak out, such as when I would offer an interpretation and he would say, "Nah, that's too easy." He was humoring me the whole time, and then waiting to make his hasty exit.

This was what his father had done to him, left suddenly without any explanation. He had seemingly been a happy-go-lucky fellow, this father, well liked by everybody. Then, when Mr. Q. was 4 years old, his father had committed suicide. They had found him in the garage, bloated with carbon monoxide. His mother had never admitted it was a suicide, and nobody in the family was ever able to discuss it. Hence Mr. Q. had never mourned his father's death.

Recognizing that Mr. Q. was not going to be dissuaded through ordinary methods of dissuasion, I decided to mirror him paradoxically. "Well, I can see that you're determined to close the door on your therapy no matter what I say. So . . ." I paused to give emphasis to my next sentence. He looked at me, waiting with eager curiosity. "Therefore, I've decided to close the door as well."

He smiled cynically. "What do you mean?"

"I mean that I'm going to make our ending mutual."

A wry smile lined his face. "That seems rather vindictive."

"Not really. I'm not doing it for revenge."

"It seems like revenge to me."

"I'm doing it, believe it or not, because I care about you."

"You seem angry to me."

"It's true, I certainly feel annoyed and disappointed that you're quitting in this way, and I'm expressing this annoyance and disappointment by taking this action. But it's not out of revenge. I want to do everything I can do to stop you from leaving therapy in a destructive way and depriving yourself of the opportunity to work through these feelings. As I said earlier, you're at a point when you can learn more than you ever have before in therapy. Everything you've worked toward in therapy is coming to a head right now, and if you simply repeat your pattern and run from this relationship as you've run from all your relationships in the past, both of us will have failed. You'll have to start all over with another therapist, and eventually you'll get to this same place again with another therapist, only you'll have had to spend a lot more money and time getting here again.

"I'm also closing the door from my side because I don't want to leave you with the assumption that you can come back to me if you want. This would merely give you the chance to go on acting out your negative transference feelings, even after you've terminated, by not coming back. And this is exactly what you will do, based on my experience with other people I've treated.

"No, I'm not doing this out of vengeance. I'm doing it because this is what I think I have to do, therapeutically. And if you still decide to leave despite it all, then so be it. At least I'll know I tried my best to keep you from sabotaging your therapy. And I won't have let you succeed at quitting without taking responsibility for it."

By the time I had finished this little speech, Mr. Q.'s face was downcast. Gone was the superior twinkle in his eyes and the wry wrinkle at the corners of his mouth. I had watched him carefully as I spoke, and had ended my speech at what I thought was the appropriate moment. Overkill would have been counterproductive.

"So you think I have negative feelings about you?" he finally asked.

"Yes."

"But I'm not aware of any."

"Don't you feel a little annoyed at me now, for threatening to close the door from my side?"

He shrugged his shoulders. "A little. It was expected. I had a feeling you'd do something."

"We seem to be in a power struggle."

"I suppose. So? Does that mean I have negative feelings about you?"

I reminded him of things that had leaked out in previous sessions, and gave him an interpretation about his passive-aggressive mode of expressing his anger and contempt for authority figures. That finally rang a bell. He recalled a former mentor of his, when he was a teenager, who had aroused such feelings. He had joined this youth organization, run by a charismatic man who seemed dedicated to helping young men find themselves. Mr. Q. was a troubled teenager who dabbled in petty thefts and in drugs. For a while he put his faith in this youth leader, even stopped some (not all) of the petty thefts and the drug-taking. Then one day the youth leader began touching Mr. Q. and then he pulled down Mr. Q.'s pants and had anal sex with him. Mr. Q. had let him do it almost out of curiosity, he said, but afterward he felt disgusted with himself and with the leader. His former cynicism about authority figures returned and he went back to his life of indulgence.

"So deep down you don't believe in any of us authority figures," I remarked. "You think we're all talking out of both sides of our mouths. We act like we're great, caring guys who'll be there for you, and then we abandon you or let you down in some way or another, like your former mentor—and like your father. You wanted to abandon me before I let you down. Is that it?"

"That's too easy," he said at first. Then, "Maybe . . ."

"Or perhaps you wanted to spare me from the direct expression of your contempt."

"Maybe . . ."

At the end of the session Mr. Q. sighed and muttered, "I guess I'll see you next week." Then the wry smile returned for just a moment. "Congratulations. You won."

"No," I said, "You won."

"I'm just kidding," he quickly added.

"Sure. So was I," I said, continuing to mirror him.

I had mirrored his threat to abandon me and the therapy process by threatening to abandon him as well. I had made him understand something that he would not have understood otherwise. I made him feel the feelings that he was provoking in me, the feelings of anger at suddenly being cut off. However, I did not mirror him exactly. Whereas he was abandoning me while professing only love and respect for me and denying he had any negative feelings (which is probably what his father did before he committed suicide), I acknowledged that I was annoyed at him for abandoning me thus and that I was taking this hard line because it was what I needed to do, therapeutically. I was modeling for him an objective form of hate. I hated him at that moment, but not with malice, not with an intent to injure. I only wanted to supply him with the antidote to his hostile, subjective form of acting out, and to show him how passive aggression could be converted to active aggression and be much more productive. Only after I had mirrored him and made him feel my own anger and my reasons for it, only then would he truly listen to my interpretations.

The following week (I saw him once a week), Mr. Q. was still wavering. He was still not sure about me or therapy. But I continued my onslaught of interpretations and by the end of the session he acknowledged having contempt for me and spoke of the stupid socks I always wore. After three more sessions he was ready to lie on the couch again (he had sat up all the while he was talking about leaving). A month later he called me up and wanted to schedule an emergency session.

The man who walked into my office the day of the emergency session was a different man than I had ever seen. His face and body were animated. "What a week I've had. After our last session, I went home and called one of my friends and I started crying. I've been crying all week. I don't know what's happening to me." The crying lasted for two weeks, and during that time his entire physical persona changed; he looked softer, younger, and confused. "What's happening? I don't understand what's happening," he muttered, looking up frightenedly. "You know how I've always hated my mother. Well, this week I started feeling very sad about her and I actually called her to apologize. I don't understand it at all."

I explained to him that by preventing him from acting out his repeating pattern with me, I had forced him to get in touch with the underlying feelings. The defensive posture of cynicism had cracked, releasing a major repression, complete with memories and feelings. The sadness and confusion he now felt was the sadness and confusion he had experienced a long time ago after his father died. He had longed for his mother's comfort then, but had not gotten it. His mother was in denial. Even today she still denied that her husband had committed suicide. To her it was an accident, and the way to deal with it, then and now, was just to forget it, to put it out of her mind and move on.

So Mr. Q.'s child's heart had opened up again and he felt loving and open to the world. He apologized to his mother and cried long-lost tears, and he cried to his women friends. The crying went on for a couple of weeks. Unfortunately, he did not get the response he had hoped for from his mother. She reacted now as she probably had done then: What was all the fuss about? Any display of emotion scared her.

Then he became sick with mononucleosis and had to do his sessions on the telephone. Once again he wanted to know what was happening. I said I thought he had somatized his feelings, and that this was again a repeat of what had happened in the past. He now remembered how as a child he had frequently been sick. This was the only way he had been able to get his mother to show any sympathy. If he had anything to say about his father, or about her, the smile of denial on her face would widen and she would change the subject. But at times of sickness she became Florence Nightingale.

Eventually he got over the mononucleosis and came regularly to his sessions. He did not return to his former defensive posture of cynicism, however, but remained more optimistic. There were still bouts of depression, but he felt the depression now rather than burying it behind the wall of cynicism. His relationships with women were a bit different; the pattern was still there, but he stayed longer in his relationships.

The work we had done had carried him forward. I had departed from standard procedure when I used the mirroring technique. But once he had decided to stay in therapy, I was able to return to standard procedure and we made great strides in interpreting his behavior. His contempt for me was still lurking there, along with the pseudo-conscientious attitude, and would yet require much working through. But he had flipped over into a positive transference. Generally, from then on, he was truly respecting and listening to me, not faking it as before, and there was more of a sense of a real camaraderie and teamwork brewing. If this sense of camaraderie happened to be what his inner child had long craved and felt cheated out of by his father, so much the better.

CHAPTER 4

Other People's Penises

Paradoxical Behavioral Techniques with a Perverse Patient

In the middle of his first session, lying flat on the couch, his red, high-top sneakers dangling over the edge, his T-shirt rising and falling as his belly bulged, looking like an adolescent cherub though he was over 30, he said, "Oh, Christ. This is embarrassing. But you said I'm supposed to say everything that comes into my mind and not censor, didn't you?"

"That's right."

"Well, what came into my mind was that I feel like jacking off. Oh, Christ. I can't believe I said that."

"What's that about?"

"I don't know. I guess it would feel good. It would be fun. I'd like to jack off in front of you, and I'd like you to see my dick, see it get hard, and then I'd like you to take your dick out and start whacking off, too. I'd like to see your dick, see how it gets hard and what method you use to whack it off, two fingers or whole hand, or whatever. Oh, Christ, this is really embarrassing. But I guess I should say all of it. In fact . . . Oh, God . . . I'm starting to get hard right now as I'm telling you about this. Well, that's it. Wheeow! That's what I was thinking about. About jacking off in front of you. Unzipping my fly and taking my dick out and jacking off.''

"How would you like me to feel about that?" I said, starting to feel a bit uneasy.

"Honestly? Of course, honestly, stupid," he muttered to himself. "That's what therapy is about. Don't mind me, I always talk to myself. Anyway, to answer your question, I guess I'd like you to feel excited." He had moved his hand down to his crotch and was almost imperceptibly rubbing his index finger against it. "Actually, I'd like it if you got a big hard-on."

"What are you doing with your finger?" I asked.

"Oh, that . . . well . . ."

This first session stated the theme, masturbation, and it would be followed by variations on the theme. Marvin was obsessed with his penis and what it could do. He was a passive phallic narcissist, stuck in the early phallic stage of development, when little boys discover masturbation. His answer to any stressful situation in his life was to find a closet, a stairway, a bathroom, or a cranny where he could masturbate. He would masturbate during the daytime and at nighttime, after his wife had gone to sleep. He would masturbate lying down or standing up. He would masturbate indoors or outdoors. He generally masturbated three or four times a day and could masturbate for hours at a time.

During the course of his treatment, his masturbation itself went in various directions. For a year or so he would masturbate privately at home or on the sly in public restrooms. Then he went through a phase where he went to pornography shops and masturbated in booths while watching pornographic movies—usually gay but sometimes straight. On occasion he would jack off while looking at a scantily dressed woman in a glass booth next to his, and on other occasions he would call up a telephone sex line, usually gay, but sometimes straight, and jack off. Then he went through a phase where he went to public restrooms and masturbated with other men. Sometimes he would do it while sitting in a booth, sometimes while standing at the urinal. During this phase he discovered an underground of men's rooms around the city where young men met and masturbated together casually, usually without exchanging a word. One was at a university; another was in a public building.

All the while, Marvin would profess to be concerned about his compulsion to masturbate. "I told myself when I left the house this morning that I didn't want to go to the restroom today and jack off," he would say. "Because I always feel guilty afterward and wonder what my wife would do if she ever found out. I mean, Christ, she's frightened to death of AIDS. Can you imagine what she'd do if she knew I was masturbating with other men in public restrooms? But, as you probably guessed, I couldn't control myself. When lunchtime rolled around, there I was at the restroom. I had to play with my dick about a half hour before somebody sat at the booth next to me. I knew by the sounds he was making he was jacking off, so after a while I peeped under the booth and watched him jack off. I found it really excited me to see the way he handled his dick. He used a two-finger technique, his index finger and thumb, whereas I use three." He lay on the couch, his legs slightly spread, his arms at his sides, at attention, as though forever expecting to be chastised. "I reached up to touch his dick at one point, but he moved away. He didn't want me to touch him and that was fine with me. I don't like to be touched either."

Touching other men did not excite him. He was primarily obsessed with mutual masturbation—with looking at other men's penises and having them look at his. If he could not do that then the next best thing was to talk about it with another male. Probably 60 percent of his therapy sessions was spent talking about his masturbation. In the beginning he attempted to justify it and prove how wonderful it was, as though he constantly expected me to tell him it was gross. "I masturbated for a half hour last night before I went to bed. My dick was rock hard," he would blurt out, and serenade me with details about how he had gotten aroused, maintained an erection, and felt at all stages. When I neither approved nor disapproved, he relaxed and supplied me with a running account of his fantasies. From these we were able to learn more about his underlying fears.

One of his first recurring fantasies was of meeting up with a witch-woman who scolded him for masturbation and then punished him by having him masturbate for one hour, which caused his penis to grow two feet long. This fantasy harkened back to the punitive mother of his early phallic stage of development, a stage during which 3-year-old boys fall in love with their own penises and proudly flaunt them before their mothers. While his mother had been scornful of his phallic exhibitionism, in this fantasy the witch herself had a penis, and so was not jealous of his penis but instead ordered him (gave him permission) to masturbate. However, like the character in the children's story, Pinocchio, his appendage grew to grotesque proportions. This expressed his unconscious wish for his mother's acceptance, and his fear that his phallic grandiosity would do him in.

In another fantasy he imagined himself, not as he actually looked, but as another man possessing the kind of large penis, muscular build, and confidence he lacked. As this other man he would have sex with a woman and satisfy her repeatedly. This fantasy compensated for his feelings of masculine inferiority.

Later, he had another fantasy in which he would walk around willing other men to masturbate. He had some kind of magical, hypnotic power to control other men's penises in these fantasies, and upon looking at them they would excuse themselves, run to the nearest bedroom or bathroom, and begin frantically and enjoyably playing with themselves. "I had a fantasy last night that I looked at President Bush while he was giving a press conference on television," he said one day, "and a minute later he suddenly excused himself and said he had to run to the bathroom to jack off. I imagined him in the White House bathroom, jerking away at his dick, a smile of glee on his face. Then I imagined that I looked around at you during our session and you pulled out your dick during the session and began whacking it."

"What happened then?"

"I pulled out my dick and we masturbated together."

"Why does that excite you?"

"Because, deep down I think every man jerks off, but they don't admit it."

"Did Bob jack off?" I asked, referring to his older brother.

"I'm sure he did, but he never admitted it."

"Did your father?"

"God, I don't know. He's so pure. I just can't imagine him masturbating. He must have, though."

"Do you think I masturbate?"

"I don't know. I hope so."

"What would it mean to you if you knew that all other men masturbated?"

"Then I'd know I wasn't the only one."

"Does that mean deep down you really think you are the only man in the world who masturbates?"

"I suppose so. I suppose deep down that's what I really feel. I know it's idiotic. But that's what I feel."

Marvin was a middle child who had a brother two years older and a sister five years younger. Marvin's parents, he found out later, had only wanted two children, a boy and a girl. The second son's arrival was a disappointment. From the beginning Marvin was compared unfavorably with his older brother. His older brother had all the right habits, did all the right things, and was popular and athletic. Marvin had all the wrong habits, was not popular, not an athlete, and though he made better grades than his older brother, he was not seen as measuring up to him in any way.

His mother seems to have been intolerant of his penis, perhaps of penises in general, which apparently caused him to develop the fixation about his penis and other people's penises. There is a stage of development that all little boys go through called the phallic narcissistic stage. It happens at around 3 or 4, when little boys become obsessed with their penises. During this stage it has been observed that little boys commonly take great pride in their penises and what they can do. A penis can magically get erect and magically produce wondrous sensations. All one has to do is pump it a few seconds and it stands up. This is something to behold, a discovery that must rank with the greatest of boyhood's many discoveries. A little boy will run to his mother upon such discoveries and say, "Look, Mom, look what my peepee can do!" If a mother is intolerant of penises, if she never resolved the envy of that organ, she may turn away in disgust, roll up her eyes, slap his hand, or in some other way indicate her disapproval. Such a reaction will arouse in the boy a mixed feeling. On the one hand he does not want to provoke his mother's disapproval; on the other hand he cannot deny the pride and pleasure his penis gives him. So he develops a conflict about his sexuality and becomes fixed at the phallic narcissistic stage.

In Marvin's case, although there was no direct memory of this phase of development, there were later memories of his mother's attitude toward his penis. He recalled, for example, that his mother became furious if he dribbled on the lid of the toilet or on the bathroom floor, carrying on for days about each such happening. Such carryings on made him feel that the products of his penis were vile and offensive as well as the organ itself. He recalled how, during puberty, when his mother saw hairs sticking out of his bathing suit, she looked away with disdain and exclaimed, "You're sticking out of your suit." He recalled how she would wince whenever she saw male ballet dancers on television. "They shouldn't wear tights, it's obscene!" she would hiss. When Marvin asked her what was obscene, she would say, "Never mind." But he and everybody knew full well what she meant.

From these clues, from what I had read in the literature, and from my experience in treating similar cases, I deduced that his mother had not given him the response he needed during the phallic narcissistic stage. The proper response would have been simply to accept these feelings without either encouraging nor repudiating him. Had she done so, he would have gone through this stage rather than getting stuck in it. She had not been able to respond properly because she herself was stuck in a stage of pregenital sexual development. She herself, I guessed, had not gotten the response she needed with regard to the discovery of her own sexual anatomy, and the normal jealousy that all little girls feel upon first discovering that little boys possess something that they do not possess had not been resolved but had instead festered. The cycles of generational parenting are made up of precisely such repeating episodes.

Marvin not only had to contend with these sexual rebukes from his mother, but also had to parry more vicious attacks from his older brother. The brother was continually teasing Marvin, making him feel that he was

stupid and ridiculous and inferior. If Marvin became upset
at his brother's attacks and ran to his mother for protec-
tion, she would become enraged. "Why can't the two of
you learn to play together without fighting? I have enough
on my mind without being further aggravated by you
two." In effect, she allowed the older brother to have his
way with Marvin, so that Marvin again developed a fixation and had to repress a large part of his real self and his
real feelings.

He and his brother would be sitting in the backseat of
the car and his brother would keep hitting or pinching
him. He couldn't fight back because if he did his brother
would overpower him.

So he would sit silently as his brother pinched or hit
him, pretending he was not there.

"Does it hurt?" his brother would taunt. "Say it. Say, 'It
hurts.' Come on, say it and I'll stop."

"No, you won't stop."

"I promise I'll stop if you say, 'It hurts.' "

"No."

"I'll bet you're going to scream in a minute."

"No."

"Go ahead, I know you want to scream."

"No."

He would sit painfully, silently, knowing if he screamed
his brother would win and his mother would yell at both
of them. No matter what he did, it was a no-win situation;
so he would sit silently and fantasize that someday he
would be a movie star and they would all be sorry.

Indeed, the mother and brother were often in cahoots
against him, as when he ran out of the bathroom in his
underwear and his older brother started laughing and
pointing at his underwear. He called the mother into the
room and said, "Look, Mom, look at that. He's got his

underwear on backward! He doesn't even know his front from his behind."

"I do, too," Marvin fiercely defended himself.

"No, you don't!"

"I do, I do, I do!"

"Can't you even put your underwear on the right way?" his mother scoffed, laughing.

And she and her older son laughed together, and Marvin went off by himself and quickly changed his underwear, determined that from that time forth he would take the greatest possible pains to put his underwear on the right way, and in fact to do everything perfectly.

And where was the father during this time? He was there but not there. He abdicated all authority to his wife. A passive male, he wished to avoid a confrontation at all costs, and in particular to avoid his wife's hysteria. Therefore, he yielded to her in every way, and never intervened on Marvin's behalf. Yet, his persona was that of a fair-minded, religious, gentle man who wanted only to do what was right, so Marvin could never fault him. Often Marvin and his father would have talks about things, and his father seemed to take him seriously. But Marvin could see that the father, like his mother, really favored the older brother, although he was making an effort to appear to be neutral.

Feeling his masculinity, his sexuality, and his very being attacked by his mother and older brother, Marvin turned to the father as he would turn to a life buoy during a hurricane. He needed a male figure to tell him that his sexual impulses, thoughts, and feelings were all right and not dirty or repulsive. But his father could not save him; in fact, he added to Marvin's difficulties.

Every evening the father would walk around the house naked, exposing his genitals to the boy, arousing Marvin's sexuality, yet not ever dealing with the boy's feelings or his own acting out. This ritual continued even after Marvin had moved away. Marvin remembered an occasion in his adolescence, when he and his father shared a hotel room, and his father showered and lay in his bed naked reading a paper. Marvin followed suit and lay in his bed also naked, reading a comic book. (He read comic books long into his adult years.) He remembered feeling excited by this nudity, as he had as a boy, but also embarrassed and awkward.

"I see the Yankees lost again," the father said, as though nakedness were nothing.

"So what else is new," the son said, thinking about his penis, and hoping it would not get erect in front of his father.

"They need a new manager," the father said.

"They need a new team," the son said, thinking that it would have been wonderful if his father had started to masturbate and he himself could have also masturbated. Father and son masturbation. Yes!

"Maybe in the next century," the father said, putting down the Sports Section and turning out the light. "Good night."

"Good night," the son said, and in the dark, quietly, he masturbated, feeling guilty, feeling inferior, hoping his father would not hear him or see the bedsheet going up and down in the dark, and hoping he would.

In households where parental nudity is a way of life (such as in homes of philosophical nudists who frequent nudist camps) and not something that is incongruous, it does not necessarily have to cause a problem. But in the case of Marvin's father, it was incongruous with his otherwise puritanical standards, something that he did each night that was never spoken about nor explained. Nobody in the house ever talked about their real thoughts or feelings about each other or what was going on between them. Hence, the nudity was an odd, stimulating undercurrent, the effect of which was denied. What is denied grows stronger.

When Marvin's younger sister was born, just as he was nearing his fifth birthday, he was abandoned. His mother and father had finally gotten the daughter they wanted. Now Marvin became not only an object of disgust to his parents, but also a nuisance, an unwanted burden, somebody they would rather not have around. By then he had already become an overweight little boy who took to food to soothe himself and who played the congenial clown in order to deflect the ridicule hurled at him. Being abandoned by his mother and excluded from participation in the nurturing of the new baby reinforced his feelings of inferiority and alienation. He became an avid reader and lived in his head.

During latency he became fatter and fatter, and his brother teased him about his weight. His mother, now busy doting on her daughter, left him to the mercy of the older brother. To protect himself, Marvin asked to move out of the room he shared with his brother, into the basement. It was a cold and dank and uncarpeted basement without windows, but at least it was peaceful. Nobody in the family understood why he wanted to move to the smelly old basement, but the parents acceded to his wishes, thinking this was just one of his oddball interests, like reading comic books. Instead, while they deprived him of their attention and love, they indulged him materially, giving him more allowance than he needed, so that he was able to have his own television set, his own stereo, and the largest collection of comic books in town.

In high school he developed an interest in the theater. By that time he had learned to be the perfect, unobtrusive son, never in any way directly confronting his family about anything. However, he had one habit that irritated and infuriated his mother. As a theater major, he had developed a British accent. Whenever he practiced the accent at home while talking to his mother, she would throw a tantrum and tell him to stop it "at once." He did not understand why the accent bothered her so much, and would keep forgetting and do it again.

"Oh, that this too too solid flesh would melt . . ."

"Stop it."

"I say, Mother dear, are you all right?"

"You just do that because you know it gets on my nerves!"

"But Ma*ma*, I dare say, I'm only practicing my Shake-speare."

She stormed out of the room.

In late adolescence he discovered his penis again, and the interest in comic books was displaced by his interest in masturbation. He spent nearly all his leisure hours masturbating in his basement "hideout" below the rest of the family. He emerged only to join them for dinner, then went back to his basement. Alone in the basement, his hand always on his penis, he could imagine things. He could imagine being a handsome movie star with the biggest penis in the world. He could imagine coming home to Alabama as a celebrity, sitting down to dinner with his family, and his older brother apologizing to him, and his parents begging his forgiveness. He could hold on to his penis and imagine anything he wanted whenever he wanted. At least nobody could tell him what he could or could not imagine.

Later as an adult he met a woman who was very much like his mother—one who had a derogatory view of masculinity and male sexuality—and he married her while in his mid-twenties. She became his mother-surrogate and he tried to be her good boy, as he had done for his mother.

In bed she would never touch his penis, nor would she allow him to touch her vagina. She was only interested in having sex in the missionary position, and felt that any other kind of sexual experience was "dirty." In the beginning, before he had had much therapy, he suffered from bouts of premature ejaculation and impotence with her, particularly at times when he felt angry at her (or someone else).

Since he had learned to swallow his anger (and, in fact, to not even be aware of it), he tended to suppress and not be aware of any irritation he felt toward his wife when she refused to touch his penis or in some other way degraded or restricted their sexual contact. In fact, his wife was the kind of woman who was always picking fights with people and demanded to have the last word. Marvin always allowed her to have the last word, and this too was a source of unconscious irritation to him. Not being aware of his frustration, the anger was acted out somatically through his sexual dysfunctions and through increased bouts of masturbation.

He still led two lives, just as he had at home. To his wife he presented the picture of a gentleman with all the correct moral and political opinions; but in his private life he continued to masturbate several times a day and frequent pornography shops and men's rooms. And in his sessions with me he talked with what appeared to be giddy pleasure about his masturbatory practices.

After three years of therapy he came in for a session one day and did not talk about masturbation. Nor did he talk about it the following session. Nor the one after that. Finally, four sessions later, toward the middle of the session, he brought it up.

"I've been deliberately not talking about masturbation for the last few sessions. Have you noticed?"

"I noticed. Why?"

"Because I just wanted to see if I could do it. It occurred to me that there has hardly been a session in the last three years when I haven't talked about it."

"That's true."

"And anyway, I've been feeling lately—well, actually for some time now, or for a while, or whatever you call a few months, I guess a few months could be said to be some time, couldn't it? . . . GET ON WITH IT, MARVIN! God! Blablablablabla! All right. I *can* say this. I really can. Anyway, I've been noticing how much I masturbate and how much I talk about it. At first it was fun to talk about it and when you just listened and accepted everything I felt encouraged to do more, so I've been going to more porno movies and more men's rooms and more porno stores and jerking off more, and it's to the point where I'm starting to feel weird. Are you following this? The other day as I was whacking away in the men's room at the college I thought, 'You idiot—what if you get caught?' Because I've started taking more and more risks. I whip it out and stand in front of the urinal whacking off and hoping that someone will come in and see me and start whacking off, too. And sometimes that works, but occasionally somebody will come in who's obviously straight and I have to pretend that I've been pissing and I'm finished. And I think about what would happen if my wife Mary found out—for Christ's sake—my mother. I'd be ruined. I'm really taking too many chances. Don't you think?"

"Yes, you are."

"And not only that, but it makes me feel, I don't know, yes, I do know but I don't want to say it. SAY IT, IDIOT! I feel like a creep. That's how I feel. There, it's out. I go to work and wonder if any of my fellow workers have any inkling of what I've been doing, and I imagine they do, that they can smell something or see something. And I go home to Mary and I feel like a traitor, like I've been betraying her. And God knows what kind of disease I may catch. I mean, what if I get AIDS? I know that's ridiculous, you can't catch AIDS from touching some guy's dick. But even so, I worry about it. I mean, it's gone too far, it seems like it's out of control. My life isn't measured out in coffee spoons, but in dicks. My dick, other guy's dicks. Dicks, dicks, dicks. Help!''

"What should I do?''

"I don't know. Yes, I do know, damn it. I was thinking about something you said a while back. You said you had been trained in hypnosis. Do you think you could hypnotize me?''

"So you want to cut down on the masturbation?''

"Yes. I want to control it; I don't want it to control me.''

"Well, there is a treatment plan that I could use, but I don't know if you could do it. It would require more dedication than anything you've ever done, and it would be the hardest thing you've ever had to do in your life.''

"I'll do it.''

"Wait until you hear what it is.'' I proceeded to explain the treatment plan to him. It was a paradoxical behavioral intervention that plugged into his fantasies. Although I am a psychoanalyst, I throw in other modalities if it is necessary, and it is often necessary. Psychoanalytic therapy works well only with a small proportion of the general population. It does not work well with addictive personalities, for example, until such time as they have overcome their addictions. Marvin's masturbation was not normal masturbation but an addiction—one that he had now finally admitted (the first step in an addict's recovery). As such I had to confront his addiction before he would be able to analyze himself.

His sexual fantasy about the witch-mother who ordered

him to masturbate represented a wish and a clue. Understanding this not only helped me to figure him out, but
also provided me with a key to his cure. He had become
fixated and obsessed with masturbation because he had
not been given the response he needed at a certain phase
of development; instead he had been rebuked. To resolve
this fixation, I determined to provide him with the antidote to this repudiation—playing the "witch" who would
give him permission to enjoy his infantile sexuality. I did
not say this to him, but instead simply explained that I was
using a hypnotic treatment plan of an indirect kind. His
unconscious would understand. I did not formally hypnotize him, but did so indirectly.

I told him that he was to listen very carefully to my
instructions and to follow them to the letter. I asked him if
he would be willing to do that. He said he would be. I
repeated this first instruction several times (a hypnotic
technique), and then said that beginning the following
Monday I wanted him to masturbate ten hours a week and
write down when, where, and how long he masturbated
and how many orgasms he had when he did so. I asked
him to note the quality of his erections (semihard, hard,
rockhard) and the length of his orgasm in approximate
seconds. I wanted to know the nature of his ejaculation—
did it squirt out or seep out—and the volume of the semen
(slight, average, heavy).

He gulped, "Really," but his cheeks were flushed and I
could tell he was excited by the prospect.

I repeated this instruction again and again in different
words. I told him that if he did not think he could do the
ten hours, then we should forget the plan, because the
plan would only work if he did it exactly as I instructed. I
said he would think of many reasons not to do the plan. It
might seem fun at first, but eventually he would get tired
of it and try to find reasons to stop. But if he stopped, the

entire plan would be for naught and he would be even worse off than before because he would hate himself for not being able to carry through with it. I said I did not want to start the plan unless I had his absolute assurance that he would not stop under any circumstances. I said it would be the hardest thing he had ever done, but if he did it he would definitely overcome his obsession with masturbation and feel much better about himself. I said his self-esteem would increase dramatically if he succeeded. I explained that masturbation was an act of rebellion, an act of spite aimed at his family. He had been put into a no-win situation by his family. Not only his masturbation, but also his very self had been under attack. He could not even complain about his situation without being further attacked. So he had moved into his basement and become a basement masturbator at night and a perfectionist during the day. Whenever things did not go well in his life, he masturbated. Whenever he had a fight with his boss or wife, he masturbated. Whenever he was insulted by friend or foe, he masturbated. If his mother called to say hello and to insist that he buy a new suit, he masturbated. If his father sent him a hefty check for his birthday, he masturbated. Masturbation was his ultimate solution, his solace, his strength, his secret of life. It was his rite of passage to manhood. So he thought. But in fact its excess was keeping him back, immature, distracted, unable to make love to his wife, mired in low self-esteem, and locked in a repeating pattern of futility. I explained all this to him and watched his eyes and his body as I did so. He was breathing slowly and his eyes were looking a bit to the side, as if to see me without looking directly at me. I could tell that he was listening to me with great intensity and that I had "droned" him into a trance. I kept talking in a monotone, repeating all of this over and over.

Then I began talking about penises. I told him that he

had been doing a lot of thinking about penises and that it was okay to think about penises, that penises were wonderful, exciting things and that many people had them and that he should feel proud to be one of them. I said there were many penises in the world, and some of them were black and some white and some yellow and some brown; I pointed out that some penises were narrow and some were long and some were short and some curved to the right and some curved to the left and some curved up and some curved down; I said that most penises had black pubic hair but that some had brown or red or blond or brunette pubic hair, and that some pubic hair was curly and some straight and some long and dangly and some short and bristly; I said that some penises had moles or birthmarks or prominent veins, and some were circumcised and some were not. I said that some penises were accompanied by long narrow testicles and some had short fat testicles. Some testicles were soft and wrinkly as dried prunes, and others were round and firm as almonds. Some testicles were supersensitive and some were not so sensitive, but I pointed out that whether a man had "balls" in the popular vernacular did not depend on the size and shape of his testicles or on how sensitive they were but on the size of his heart.

I assured him that not only did President Bush have a penis but that every president of the United States had had a penis, as did all the male leaders of all the countries of the world. Even Napoleon had had a penis, I told him, although he did not have a penis any more. Napoleon's penis was floating in a jar in New Jersey. It had been removed from him upon his death in 1821 on St. Helena's Island and was on view at a small roadside museum. He could go look at it if he wanted, I said, but it was actually quite an ordinary and somewhat smallish penis of the uncircumcised variety. You could not tell by looking at

Napoleon's penis how often or with what method he masturbated, but I was sure he masturbated often, particularly before and after battles. Maybe he even masturbated with some of his officers before each battle, as a kind of masculine ritual, or had his officers masturbate in front of him so that he could study their penises. Of course, I was only speculating about this, I said, and I did not really know what Napoleon or Caesar or Alexander the Great did with their officers, but penises were certainly fascinating and it was fun to speculate about other people's penises, was it not?

I assured him that most of the great men of the world had masturbated at one time or another, although, like his brother and father, they pretended that they did not. I said that from the birth of the first man to the present time over six billion males of the species *Homo sapiens* had inhabited the earth and that nearly all six billion had masturbated. Even now as I was speaking there were probably millions of men masturbating, and I suggested that he could see all of them in his mind's eye if he wanted, see millions of hands on millions of erect and semierect penises, noting which of them used the thumb and two-finger method and which used the three- or four- or five-finger mode. Probably a great many in this throng of whacking-off men had been told by their mothers and sisters and older brothers that they were despicable and that their penises were despicable but they masturbated anyway and with much zest. And we are only talking about the males on earth, I added, whereas if we included all the males of the universe, then the number of whacking off males would be infinite, zillions and zillions of penises everywhere, blue and green and purple penises with stripes and polka dots and strange nodules and crevices.

Penises are beautiful, I told him, and they can do many things and some can stay erect for a long time and some for a shorter time, but you have to keep them covered because some males in the Arctic region have been known to suffer from penile frostbite. I told him it was all right for him to masturbate because that kept his penis warm and it was also good for his circulation and kept his weight down. It was also all right to think about penises, I told him, and that not only should he masturbate 10 hours a week but he should spend most of the remaining time thinking about his penis and his father's penis and his brother's penis and Napoleon's penis and any penis he cared to think about. Nobody could tell him what penis to think about or when to masturbate or whether to masturbate standing up or lying down. I reminded him that his father had an interesting penis and his brother had a stupid penis but his mother and sister did not have penises. I said that he had seen his father's penis often when he had strolled about the house naked and his testicles had swung about as he walked and the shaft of his penis was powerful and the head gleamed in the moonlight or lamplight, and I did not know if it curved up or down or sideways or what kind of pubic hair it had or how firm the testicles were. Only *he* knew these details. As for his brother, I suspected that his penis was not as big as Marvin imagined, and I did not think it was shiny like his father's. Probably his own penis was now bigger than his brother's, perhaps even bigger than his father's, the shaft mightier, and the head taller.

I told him I had once known somebody who had a smiling penis, yes, a penis that looked like a smiling face, with two dimples on the cheeks, and I assured him that his penis could be smiling too after he did this plan, after he followed my instructions to the letter and masturbated 10 hours a week. I told him his penis was his own business, not his mother's, not his father's, not his sister's, not his brother's, and that it did not matter whether his mother or his wife approved or disapproved of his penis or its mysterious workings. It was his penis and only his, to do with what he wished, and if that made others jealous that was their problem. His penis could pee a golden stream and if his sister and mother and others of the female gender could not do so with their vaginas, then that was their problem. His penis could fit nicely into his whole hand and pulsate with life, and if his sister and mother could not grab their vaginas and make them do things, that was their problem. He did not have to feel ashamed or guilty. He had a fine penis and it could do many things and until now he had had to keep it a secret to himself, keep its magical powers out of sight, and perform in secret rebellion. I said I knew that his penis was his solitary covert strength, and I congratulated him about it.

I continued like this long after a normal person would stop, repeating many sentences again and again. I wanted to saturate him with penis talk and with plans for masturbatory activity. This was my answer to his phallic narcissism. At the age of 3 or 4 his pride in his penis and in his masculinity had been met by scorn, so the normal narcissism of that stage had congealed into a lifelong narcissistic shell of pride and defiance that acted as an umbrella, shielding his obsession and compulsion. His narcissism had been attacked and now he had spent his life defending and perpetuating it. His cherubic body, his red high-top sneakers, his comic books (transitional objects) all harkened back to his fixation in a pregenital stage. To break through this defensive shell and forestall the repeating pattern, I had to join it. On one level I was the primal witch giving him permission and acceptance he had sought from his "witch" mother, whom he had separated from his "real" mother in his fantasies; on another level I was the empathic father he had needed to validate his masculine strivings; and on yet another level I was his alter ego, joining his obsession about penises and masturbation by providing him with a commentary that was just as obsessive as his own thoughts and fantasies. By doing this I could show him that I understood the depth of his obsession and that, indeed, I could be just as obsessed, just as compulsive, and it was all right. The more detailed my induction was, and the more it matched his own thoughts or perception, the more effective it would be.

Finally, after spending the session inducing him, I asked, "Well, what do you think?"

"It sounds fun!" he answered right away. "I can't wait to get started. I'll probably go somewhere and whack off as soon as I leave."

"Do it!" I said like a cheerleader. "Do it!"

After the first week, he came back beaming excitedly. "It was great. I had permission to do what I love to do." His notes about his masturbation, giving details of all aspects of his practices as I had instructed, were copious.

After the second week, he came back sighing. "It was getting a little bit tiring this week. I wanted to stop in the middle because my penis was sore and I was feeling a bit self-conscious. I must confess I was a tad resentful toward you." His notes were not as copious.

After the third week, he came back wincing. He had no notes for me. "I'm feeling extremely angry at myself," he said, lying stiffly and agitatedly on the couch. "As you've probably realized, I couldn't finish. I stopped the program last Wednesday. So shoot me!"

"Why are you angry at yourself?"

"Because I'm a failure. I couldn't do it." His narcissistic perfectionism had been broken.

"Why aren't you angry at me?" I asked. "I'm the one who gave you an impossible task to do."

"As a matter of fact, I am angry at you."

"Tell me about it."

He did, and the therapy took a sharp turn for the better. As the result of the treatment plan, his masturbation had become a job rather than a joy, an act of duty rather than of rebellion. He felt silly, ashamed, and weak as he did it. It affected the way he was doing his job, the way he related to his wife. When he could no longer get erect for his wife and was concerned about his sore penis, he backed off from the plan. Having failed, he found himself feeling enraged at his brother and his parents, then at me. The shell was cracked and the repeating pattern derailed. The anger that had been acted out in this obsessive act of masturbatory rebellion now came to the surface and was directed at its source and at me in the transference. I accepted it and analyzed it. A new, more authentically emotional bond was formed between us. He listened to me now with both ears and no longer tried to get me to masturbate with him. Instead, he joined with me (as I had joined his obsession) in the pursuit of analysis. No, he did not live happily ever after, but he masturbated with less obsession and loved better.

CHAPTER 5

An Asinine Obsession

Joining Techniques to Break an Obsession

Session after session, week after week, he would wander in late, flop haplessly on the couch, and utter the same litany.

"I don't feel like talking."

"How come?"

"It won't do any good."

"Why won't it?"

"Because it won't."

"Last week you said you were feeling better."

"I don't remember."

"What happened since last week?"

"I don't want to think about it."

"Why don't you want to think about it?"

"Thinking doesn't help."

"You can't figure things out?"

"That's right."

"Why?"

"Because I'm a loser. I'm hopeless. I'm a creep. I'm a jerk. I'm a wimp. My ears are too big, I have a gap between my teeth, and my lips are too thick. I'm ugly and I'm stupid. I don't deserve anything good. The best thing for me is to stay locked up in my apartment and not inflict

myself on the world. I'm an asshole. I'm a prick. I should
never have been born. The one thing I can always depend
on is that I'll always screw up. . . ."

"What happened? Did you see Louisa?"

"Yeah. I saw Louisa. How did you guess?"

"Where did you see her this time?"

"On the subway platform."

"Did she see you?"

"I'm not sure. I thought she did, but when I smiled at
her she just looked away."

"Did you try to talk to her?"

"No. I walked down to the end of the platform and got
on a different car."

"That's it?"

"That's it."

Dick could go on like this for most of the session,
negating himself and negating me and dwelling on his
relationship with Louisa. For two years he had obsessed
about her and for two years he had been comfortably
miserable in his obsession, full of warm self-doubt and
wistful self-loathing. It was an obsession that he loved to
hate and one from which neither friend nor therapist
could pry him loose. The irony was that far from being the
ugly duckling he made himself out to be, he was a handsome man in his thirties with soft brown eyes and an
athletic build; but his depressive attitude was such that he
carried himself as though he were ugly and so that is
largely how the world saw him.

He would nearly always slink into my office with the
sulky look of an awkward little boy, his face wrinkled with
gloom, as though he were saying, "I'm worthless." During
the sessions he would go in and out of a twilight state; one
minute he would be degrading himself or bemoaning his
fate with Louisa, and the next he would fall silent and I
would know he was asleep.

"Hello?" I would call.

"Hummm . . ."

"Should I let you sleep?"

"What? . . . I don't know. What was I just saying?"

"You were talking about Louisa."

"Oh."

"You don't remember talking about Louisa?"

"No . . . I don't remember anything. . . ."

"You had run into Louisa in the subway."

"I don't remember. . . ."

"Don't you want to talk about Louisa?"

"To hell with Louisa."

"Dick?"

"What? . . ."

"You're supposed to talk during sessions?"

"I don't want to talk. . . ."

"Why don't you talk?"

"Hmmmmm . . ."

His days were spent in the same twilight state. He was of that Manhattan breed for whom existence means to go to work and go home. Relationships were to him an unfathomable maze. Bosses, teachers, or any other authority figures were out to manipulate and control him. Friends could only be superficially trusted. Relationships with women were few and fleeting. His dearest confidant was not any human being—least of all me—but his diary. Indeed, often when he would come in not wanting to talk, he would say, "Why should I tell you? I'd rather write it in my diary. At least my diary won't say anything stupid to me."

In group therapy I found that sometimes I could help him get in touch with the deep sadness, despair, and rage inside him. Utilizing a Gestalt technique, I would have him sit opposite one of the women in the group (who invariably developed feelings of contempt for him that mirrored the contempt he felt for himself), and have him say, "I need love."

He would protest for a few minutes, but eventually he would look in the woman's eyes and say it: "I need love." Then he would shrug his shoulders and shake his head. "I don't feel anything. What is love? I don't know what it is. It's an alien thing to me."

"Say it again and mean it."

"I need . . . love . . ."

"Again."

"I need . . . I need . . ."

"Keep looking at her eyes."

"I can't . . ."

"Do it anyway. Say it. I need love."

"I need . . . love . . ."

"What do you feel?"

"Nothing."

"Say it again."

"I . . . I . . . I . . ." Finally his eyes would fill with tears and he would begin to sob like an infant, heaving from some primitive place deep inside. "I do! I do need love! Oh God, I need love! Oh God, oh God . . ." He would cry and cry, and it always seemed that there was a bottomless reservoir of sadness that could never be relieved.

These breakthroughs would plunge him into a regressed state for a few days, and he would come to his next individual session looking at me with eyes that seemed to plead not just for love, but for me to hold him in my arms and rock him for about ten years. When he did not get such a response from me, he would suddenly flip back into the numbing bitterness and despair, more deeply than ever. If I reminded him about the experience in the group he would scoff, as though it had all been a silly dream.

"Love? I don't need it. How can you need something if you don't know what it is? Anyway, it's too . . . messy. It

makes you feel too weak. It makes you feel . . . lost."
Because of the severe neglect and abuse that he had
encountered in his infancy with respect to getting love, he
now shrank back from it in terror. "Why would I need
something I've never had?"

Desperately he would attempt to get some semblance of
love by engaging in brief relationships with women that
seldom lasted beyond the first sexual experience. "I know
how to act like the kind of man women want," he would
tell me. "Having had two sisters, I know what women are
looking for. They want somebody who will listen to them
and won't put any pressure on them for sex. So I play that
role and I'm good at it. I'm damn good at it." He was
sometimes successful in getting women to bed, and
bragged about his sexual prowess when he did. "I don't
mind telling you she was really excited. That's one place
where I have no problems—in bed." As he told me about
his sexual encounters, he would reach down and scratch
or reposition his genitals, as though they were too large
and encumbering to fit in his pants. "We must have done
it three times in an hour. She was really getting off. Then
I reverted to my old pattern." His pattern was that after
having sex with them, he would feel disgusted and find
some excuse to reject them. They had either smelly breath
or smelly feet or a smelly vagina. They either wore the
wrong kind of clothes or had the wrong kind of laugh.
They were either too tall or too short. At any rate, he
could not wait to get away from them.

Often these women would then write him letters or call,
wanting to talk, wanting to find out what was the matter,
but he would not talk, would not ever, ever allow himself
to be vulnerable to a woman. He just wanted out. At such
moments he was aware only of this intense disgust for
them and for everything about them that was feminine:
their breasts were "ugly, veiny protuberances," their

vaginas were "rotten, filthy holes," and their menstruation was "the rot that comes out of the hole, like the slime that comes out of an infested wound."

In the cases when he could not succeed with women, the pool of disgust that always reeled inside him would get turned on himself. "I blew it again," he would say, lying dejectedly on the couch.

"What happened?"

"You know that woman at the health club who kept smiling at me? Well, she now hates me."

"How so?"

"The same routine. When she was interested, I acted distant and cavalier. When she stopped being interested I became interested, only by then it was too late. She was already angry at me. It's the same pattern that happened with Louisa in the beginning." If a woman showed interest in him, and especially if she slept with him, she was disgusting—because she had allowed herself to fall for a disgusting creep like him. If a woman rejected him and did not sleep with him she was admirable, because she knew what a disgusting creep he was and avoided him. It was not sexual dysfunction that impeded him; his genitals worked fine but his heart was in constant retreat and his mind in constant distrust.

Louisa was one of those who had rejected him, and, for reasons we were not immediately able to understand, he could not get over her. It generally took him a month or so to get over a rejection, but in her case it had gone on for two years. It had started like most relationships. He had seen her in his office building, made some casual passing remarks and gotten her attention and interest. After getting her interest he choked. She saw him on the elevator, smiled, and expected him to be as friendly as he had been on previous occasions, but instead he continued talking to a colleague and all but ignored her. What he felt inside was panic. "What do I do now that she likes me?" What he showed was what he called his cavalier attitude. Thereafter Louisa was cool to him when he tried to revert to the casual charm.

For two years he had attempted to get things started again with her, trying to catch her eye when their paths crossed in the building, on the street, or in the subway. She had remained cool, most often ignoring him, sometimes acknowledging him with one-word replies, and occasionally gazing at him across a street with an ambiguous Mona Lisa smile. During his sessions with me he would speak of her beauty, her class, her intelligence, her perceptiveness, her strength, and it was clear that she had become some superwoman in his eyes, some almost omniscient creature who could handle any situation and knew everything about Dick and how to fix what ailed him. He continually bemoaned losing her and many of his utterances began with the words, "If only . . . ." By the end of many sessions he would be disparaging himself again in what appeared to be a ritual of self-flagellation. When he was through disparaging himself he would turn to me. He had several ways of punishing me—coming late, paying late, degrading me, and generally resisting all my efforts to reach him.

"I don't feel I'm making any progress," he would say.

"Am I helping you make progress?"

"No."

"How can I help you make progress?"

"You can't."

"Why can't I?"

"Because nobody can help me. I'm beyond help."

"Do you want to be helped?"

"No."

"Then how can I or anybody help you?"

"You can't."

"Then why are you here?"

"I don't know. Maybe you've brainwashed me."

"How have I done that?"

"I don't want to talk about you. You're always trying to get me to talk about my parents or about you. I'm not interested in talking about them. I'm not interested in talking about you. I'm interested in solving my problems with women."

"You've said in the past I'm not the right therapist for you. That I'm not somebody you can look up to," I persisted.

"That's true. I can't look up to you. I'm sorry. I think you want me to like you and look up to you, but I just can't. Your clothes are so cheap-looking and shabby, and your office, well, let's just say it's not on Park Avenue. And, quite frankly, you're not a cool person. You seem too vulnerable to me. Like you're having trouble in life yourself."

"In fact, you view me with the same kind of revulsion that you often feel for women you've had sex with."

"I don't know if I'd go that far. There's a big difference here. We haven't had sex."

"No, but in a sense I've given in to you. I've accepted you. I want you to work on a relationship with me, the way women do after you've slept with them. I'm interested in looking at and analyzing our relationship. And that makes you have contempt for me."

"It seems a bit farfetched. But I can see what you're saying."

"So, if you and I can work through our revulsion toward me, then maybe you'll be able to do so with a woman."

"Not unless you grow a vagina."

It was a struggle to get him to talk about his parents, much less to experience the anger he only vaguely felt toward them but transferred onto me and others in his present life. His depression and his passive-aggressive defense mechanism had, of course, been developed in response to their style of parenting, and his conditioning had been thorough; he had learned that he was required to play the role of the ''jerk,'' and that they would tolerate no other behavior from him. Every now and then he would come up with a memory or dream that indicated the depth of his ambivalence toward them, but no sooner had he told me the memory or dream than he would run away from it.

"Hello? Hello?" I would call out.

"What? . . . I must have dozed off again. What was I talking about. I can't remember what I was talking about. I can't remember a damn thing."

Dick was born to a middle-class Catholic family that lived in a large industrial city in the Midwest. His father was a frustrated white-collar worker for an automobile manufacturer, his mother was a housewife. He was the oldest of four children; two sisters and a brother followed close behind him. He attended public schools.

From the beginning he was a disappointment to his parents. His mother had told him again and again, with obvious scorn in her voice, that his eyes were crossed and his ears stuck out like donkey ears when he was born. "I don't remember either of my parents ever complimenting me in any way," he often reiterated. "Nor was there any physical contact. My mother never hugged me, and my father hardly looked at me. Later, when I went to school, the other students also treated me like an untouchable. And if I had any problems at school my parents would shrug or shake their heads as if to say, 'Well, what could we expect from such an ugly kid?' "

Dick's mother suffered from depression. She had cut herself off completely from her family of origin and had few friends. Her depression came across to Dick as a general resentment of and contempt for him. A mother's initial attitude toward a child is all-important. Her early mirroring is crucial to an infant's development of self-esteem and a cohesive self. When an infant looks into his mother's eyes, her eyes become a mirror of himself; how she sees him, he will see himself. If from the beginning he sees hate or murderous intentions in her eyes, the infant may then begin life by hating and "murdering" himself. Such apparently was the case with Dick.

He recalled not only neglect but also physical abuse. Once his arm was broken. He did not remember how it happened, but he did remember that it was days before his mother was willing to take him to a doctor. Each time he complained that the arm hurt and that it was broken, she would tell him he was making too much of things and dismiss his complaints. "How could you possibly know your arm is broken?" she chortled. Years later, after he remembered this incident in therapy, he called his mother to ask her about it. Her immediate response was to chortle and say, "You think you were an abused child, is that it?"—as though the mere idea was ridiculous.

Such, apparently, was her relationship with her oldest child. On the one hand, she neglected, deprived, and abused him, and on the other hand she would laugh at or dismiss any complaint and make him feel that any negative feelings he was having about her were simply a sign of his own sickness. He was given the message, again and again, that he was ridiculous, stupid, bad, ugly, and a general disappointment. At the same time his two younger sisters were treated quite differently. They were accorded a great deal of respect and consideration, and in time they joined with their mother and took a derisive attitude toward their brother. He could not help but notice this double standard, but he had to dismiss it from his awareness, for he was not allowed to voice any such observations in the household without being laughed at and told he was imagining things.

After his mother had her hysterectomy, she again sank into a deep depression, and once again her oldest son bore the brunt of the negative force of her depression. He recalls how for several years, during his elementary school period, he would get up in the morning to find her in bed, and come home from school and again find her in bed. He wanted desperately to help her to feel better so that she could be a better mother for him. But whenever he approached the bed to offer sympathy or support, she would bitterly attack him.

"Mom, why don't you get up and walk around."

"No."

"Maybe it would do you good."

"Nothing will do me any good."

"Can I do something?"

"No, you can't do anything. Nobody can do anything. Just leave me alone."

"Mom, I love you."

"Don't be ridiculous."

"I'm not being ridiculous."

"Yes you are. Just leave me alone."

"But Mom . . ."

"I said, leave me alone."

When he began having problems at school with a group of boys who teased and picked on him, there was nobody for him to turn to about it. His mother was always depressed, lying in the dark in her bedroom, usually with the door closed, and his father was concerned with his mother and unwilling to pay attention to the son. Indeed, his mother only made matters worse. If his report cards indicated that he was having problems getting along with other kids, no attempt was made to find out how he was feeling; instead, he was simply scolded and told that it was his fault and that he was an embarrassment to the family. When he brought home class pictures, she and his father would always comment on how his ears were sticking out or the gap between his teeth was showing or his lips were so big. Because she was always in bed, there was nobody to help him with such everyday matters as eating and dressing. His shirts were never ironed and were often missing buttons or torn; this became an additional source of teasing at school. In reaction to this, he developed an obsession, at a very early age, with his attire. He began using his meager allowance to buy shirts, and he would iron them himself.

He recalled that one day his mother got out of bed and saw him ironing one of the shirts he had picked out himself. "Are you going to wear that?" she said.

"Yes, I am."

"But your red shirt looks so much better on you."

"I don't want to wear the red shirt."

"Why not?"

"I like this shirt." He did not want to tell her that the boys had teased him about the torn sleeve on the red shirt, because then she would accuse him of saying she was a bad mother, which was the worst thing he could do.

"Wear the red shirt. Here, I'll get it," she insisted.

"I don't want to."

"You're so asinine."

He looked at her, stunned. In his mind, he had heard her say "asshole." "I'm not an asshole," he said, fighting back tears.

"Not asshole. *Asinine*. You can't even hear correctly."

"Yes I can."

"Right. Whatever you say. I don't know what to do

with you. I really don't know.'' She dragged off to the bathroom, the room in which she spent the second-most time, after the bedroom.

This antagonistic mother–son relationship continued throughout his boyhood, and was laced with teasing sexual overtones. The little physical contact that existed between them had a teasing, flirtatious quality, as when she would slide up next to him as he was watching television and put her legs on his lap, grinning. He hated it when she put her legs on his lap and she knew that; the smell of her feet disgusted him. Still, she persisted in doing it.

''Mom, stop it.'' He would push her feet away.

''Why?'' She would put them back.

''I said stop it.''

''Oh, don't be such a grouch.''

''I'm not a grouch. I just don't like your feet on my lap.''

''You're a grouch.''

He would have to move to another chair, and she would chuckle and shake her head. On its own, this interaction might not seem significant, but seen in the context of her overall relationship to him, this insistence of putting her legs on his lap was like adding insult to injury. It was another way of telling him his feelings did not matter, and it also aroused feelings in him of an aggressive-sexual kind that left him confused and enraged. For if there was no other affectional or physical bond between mother and son, nor a bond of mutual respect, than these foot touchings took on a sinister meaning. It was as though she were saying to him, ''You're not worth hugging or respecting, but you serve as a fine footrest or sex slave.'' The teasing smile that accompanied these touchings, and the fact that they were the only time she ever touched him, gave them their erotic flavor.

In the transference, Dick often showed a repugnance

toward me that represented a resurrection of the feeling state that must have existed between he and his mother. His mother would not let him help her, and he would not let me help him. His mother complained about him, calling him asinine. He complained about me. He would speak of it being too hot or stuffy in my office (stinky like his mother's feet), or express distaste for my furniture, my clothing, and even my vocabulary. Something about his tone and manner would induce in me a desire to tease him, to make fun of his complaints as his mother had. Each time he made such a statement, I would examine these countertransference feelings and understand not only the maternal transference but also what the quality of their relationship had been like.

Dick's father was equally rejecting. A passive man, he basically followed the mother's lead. If she laughed at his ears, then he laughed, too; if she saw him as asinine, he did, too; if she refused to give him physical affection, he refused, too. He remembered coming home from school in tears and throwing himself on his bed. He would stay there for hours and nobody would come to find out what was the matter. After a while he might get up and approach his Dad in hope of getting some desperately needed sympathy or respect.

"Dad," he would say, standing next to his chair, his face crunched up in pain.

His father's eyes would stay on the paper. "What?"

"They took my books and threw them in a mud puddle."

"Are they ruined?"

"No. They'll dry out, I think."

"That's good."

"Dad?"

"What?"

"Why do they keep picking on me?"

"Because you let them."

"I don't let them. They're bigger than me."

"I told you to walk the other way, but you never listen."

"I did walk home the other way."

"Well, you must have done something to make them pick on you. People don't pick on people for no reason."

The father kept reading his paper and Dick eventually crept back to his room. The father was a man who "sucked up" to everybody around him—his boss, his wife, his priest, his friends. He was submissive and needful of approval himself, and had no empathy for his son's similar needs. When it came to his son, he was disapproving, unyielding, and unable to give him any kind of empathy or guidance.

The father and mother seemed to have two personalities, one private and one public. Privately they were cold and grumpy and scornful. Publicly they were warm and outgoing. Dick recalled how every Sunday at Mass both would be the very picture of goodness, and how whenever guests came to the house they would both bubble over with good nature. What particularly galled him was that when he brought his own friends over to the house both parents would go out of their way to be gracious, bestowing on them the respect and attention he wished he could get from them. Indeed, his mother would be so vivacious with his male friends that he would feel jealous, and often she would make a point of praising one of his male friends: "That Bill is such a handsome young chap and seems to have a real head on his shoulders." Later his friends would tell him what great parents he had, and he would only shrug his shoulders and sink deeper into his isolation.

The parents themselves had gotten similar treatment from their parents. The mother, according to Dick, had broken off her relationship with her parents before Dick was born and never mentioned them. The father saw his family, but relations were strained. Generation after generation, we replicate the same faulty patterns of relating, going about our lives in a trance, making up reasons for why we do things that have nothing to do with the real reasons why we do things. We say, "I don't like this child because he has big ears," but in reality we don't like him because he is a male and we are angry at our father or our brother and the infant becomes a substitute for this deeper hate. Now and then somebody wakes up from the trance (Laing 1971) and says, "Wait a minute, this is crazy. I'm being abused," and the other family members, who have been ordered by their hypnotists (their parents) not to reveal anything, will reply, "*You're* crazy. You're seeing things. Everything's fine."

Hence, Dick's parents would treat him cruelly without knowing they were doing so, rationalizing that they had to treat him that way because he was "a bad seed," an asinine boy who needed negative attention. If he complained that they were nicer to his friends or his younger siblings, they would tell him that they would be nicer to him if he behaved better. If he said he behaved badly because he was not getting what he needed from them, they would tell him he was twisting things around as he always did. They could not take responsibility for their treatment of him and never connected their treatment of him to their feelings about their own families of origin.

So the years passed and Dick learned to bottle his feelings up and displace them. When his sisters came, he found an outlet for his bottled up frustration. He became particularly sadistic toward the older of his two sisters. He was always playing tricks on this sister, mimicking her, sneaking in her room to scare her, crawling under her bed to jump her, pinching her arms, pinning her down, and making her say, "I give up," or a code word, "Dixen." (In analyzing the meaning of this code word, it turned out that Dick was a boy at the time Richard Nixon was president, and the word was a combination of vixen and Nixon.) If this sister was sitting in the living room watching a program on television, he would menace her by running up and turning the dial. He did not really have anything else to watch, he just did not want to let her enjoy her own program.

"I was here first," she would scream. "Turn it back."

"Make me."

"Turn it back, you jerk."

"Nope."

"You're such a jerk."

"I don't care."

"You'll be sorry. I'm going to tell."

"Go ahead, Dixon. Dixon, Dixon, Dixon."

"Don't call me that."

"Dixon, Dixon, Dixon."

She would invariably tell the parents, who would yell at Dick or spank him or ground him.

No matter what he did to her, the brunt of the family aggression was always directed at him. Nor were his relations with the younger sister and younger brother any better. The younger sister, identifying with her mother, developed a similar cold and rejecting attitude toward Dick, while the younger brother was condescending. This younger brother was idealized by the parents, which directly contrasted with the scorn with which they treated Dick. Eventually, since constructive expression of anger was prevented on all sides, he developed a passive-aggressive mode of expression. He would torture his parents by asking seemingly innocuous questions until they became irritated with him. He would fight with his siblings. He would mess up at school. And twice he smashed up his father's cars.

"What the hell's the matter with you!" his father would yell at him when he wrecked the cars. "Have you got your head up your ass? You can't do anything right! I can always depend on you to do the most stupid and idiotic thing!"

Outwardly he felt humiliated by such diatribes, but inwardly there was a sense of triumph. If he could not get love and respect, then at least he could get some attention and emotional response in this indirect way.

"I saw Louisa today."

"Where did you see her this time?"

"In the lobby of my office building."

"What happened?"

"Nothing."

"What did she say?"

"Nothing."

"What did you say?"

"Nothing."

"That sounds exciting."

"I don't know why I can't just forget her."

That was the question that haunted him, and no matter what kind of answer I gave him, it did not register. Week after week he kept moping into my office asking the same question. Sometimes I would reply that he was obsessed with Louisa because he had not yet resolved his mother fixation. I would explain that he was attracted to women who scorned him, and if they did not scorn him when he met them he would get them to scorn him eventually by behaving in a contemptuous fashion toward them. Not only was he attracted to scornful women, but they also had to resemble his mother physically—that is, they had to have brown hair, brown eyes, and have a dark complexion. And it helped if they had a teasing quality in their manner.

He wanted to meet a scornful woman and somehow break through her scorn and persuade her to accept and love him. This desire harkened back to the fixation that had been forming during the period right after his mother had had her hysterectomy, when he had felt so rejected by her. He had never been able to break through his mother's scorn nor even to begin to persuade her to accept and love him, so his life's mission was to do this with another scornful woman. The problem was that scornful women seldom were accepting and loving, and if by some miracle he did manage to turn some woman's attitude around, he would then quickly lose interest in her.

Looking at him analytically, I saw him as a man with a weak, almost nonexistent ego. Since he had been scorned from birth on, he never received the ego support he needed to develop those functions for himself—he never learned to soothe himself, to tolerate frustration or feelings, to mediate between his internal conflicts or between himself and the outside world, to test reality, or to accept the blows of fate without his self-esteem plummeting. His harsh superego injunctions (the internalized scornful voices of his parents) vied with the id impulses (the little boy who was never accepted and who demanded everything now); hence his transference toward me fluctuated from the guilt-ridden confessor to passive–aggressive enfant terrible. His management of aggression was quite primitive.

He utilized the defense mechanisms of splitting and of identification with the aggressor. His depression and his continual attacks on himself and self-sabotaging behavior represented an identification with his mother, and, to a lesser extent, his father. He tended to split off the bad mother and bad father and idealize the good mother and father. Similarly, in his transference with me he tended for long stretches to idealize me, and then, for brief periods, to villainize me. The drive organization that underpinned his obsession was fueled by pregenital fixations. Both libidinal and aggressive strivings were blunted by his defenses and by his high degree of narcissism. If he could not act according to his ego-ideal (Franklin Roosevelt), he could not act at all. Hence both libido and aggression were primarily directed at the self and rarely got directed externally in any substantial way. His primary sexual act was masturbation and his main aggressive act was self-negation. Externally, libidinal strivings were limited to occasional compulsive-erotic spurts, in which the sex object became simply a narcissistic selfobject (Kohut 1971) and aggression sneaked out passively.

All of this came to bear in forming his obsession toward Louisa. His development was immature and object relations, both internal and external, remained at a level delimited by his high degree of pathological narcissism. Underlying this narcissism was his rage—the rage that his mother's scorn had evoked during the period following her hysterectomy. His mother had been alternately rejecting and pseudo-accepting (resting her feet on him), and now he was getting the same signals from Louisa. This aroused the narcissistic rage, and this rage was at the core of his obsession. The rage manifested itself in a stubborn unwillingness to let go of her. In his infantile self he was making a last stand against his rejecting mother. "Not this time, Mom," he was saying. "Not this time."

Louisa was the ideal "scornful woman." She was a dark-complexioned brunette, was slightly older than Dick, and would sometimes smile at him teasingly. The fact that she had been interested in him in the beginning and then he had lost her added more fuel to the obsession. We become most obsessed about those losses for which we feel most guilt or regret.

I would tell him all this over and over, and often he would say, "That sounds right," and he might even leave the session with a thoughtful or determined expression on his face, but the next session he would be back into the obsessive mode. Finally, I decided that the way to break the obsession was to join it. I wanted to make the obsession even bigger so that it might pop like a boil. I began encouraging him to talk about her, to fantasize about her, to dream about her. We practiced lines he might say to her if he approached her. We scrutinized her every gesture or word and analyzed her every possible motivation. In joining his obsession, I was acting differently than either of his parents, who had both repudiated him and all his thoughts, fantasies, and feelings. Moreover, I was now joining him with an ardor that outmatched even his own. In fact, I began to feel a bit obsessed with her myself. She became more and more fascinating to me, and I could not wait for his sessions so that I could find out the latest news about her. My preoccupation with her became so great that at times he would look back at me as if to say, "What's with him?" This ardor was calculated to get him to stand up and take notice of his obsessive behavior. I was not only joining him but also mirroring him, showing him what he looked like. By showing him, rather than telling him, I was able to reach the pregenital, nonverbal infantile self inside of him, wherein his chief fixation lay.

One day I asked him to have a fantasy of what it would be like to be married to Louisa, wanting to further prod him out of the obsessive thinking into something more expansive.

"I've never thought about that," he said.

"You've never thought about what it would be like to live with her?"

"No."

"What have you thought about?"

"What it would be like to fuck her."

"Well, what about after you fuck her?"

"I never get that far."

"Well, fantasize about it now. Suppose you're married to her and you come home from work and there she is in your apartment. What happens?"

"I walk in the door and she ignores me."

"How come?"

"She's angry at me."

"Oh."

"She complains that I don't care about her."

"What do you do?"

"I sit in a chair and read the newspaper."

"What does she do?"

"She sits in a chair and watches television."

"That sounds a lot like your parents."

"Yes."

"What are you feeling?"

"Closed off, sad, angry."

"What's that about?"

"I don't feel she'll ever love and accept me the way I need to be. She'll never be able to love and accept my inner child."

"You see, this fantasy explains why you can't get started with women, and why you remain obsessed with Louisa. You expect her to reject you as your mother did, particularly after her hysterectomy, and so you're paralyzed. The irony is that you're attracted to rejecting women. So you keep repeating this pattern."

I kept joining his obsession, encouraging the fantasies

about it, listening attentively to the details of his "encounters" with her, and offering interpretations. Months went by and nothing seemed to change. Actually, something was happening, but it was happening under the surface, as is so often the case in therapy—and also in life. The primary clue that something was happening came one day when he began berating himself as usual, but this time I noticed that the whine had left his voice. Instead he was outright angry at himself.

"You jerk. You creep. You simpering fool. I can always depend on you to do exactly the stupidest things. If you have a choice between an intelligent and a stupid thing, you'll do the stupidest thing every time. I can depend on it. It's like clockwork." He went on and on like this and as he spoke, I recalled that he had often quoted his father as saying almost this exact thing to him. All at once I broke in on him with a Gestalt technique.

"Try saying that to your father."

He paused and got his breath. "I know what you're saying, that I should be externalizing this anger, rather than taking it out on myself. But I just don't feel it."

"You still haven't woken up completely. You still haven't woken up from the trance your parents put you into."

"I guess so. I guess that's it. I'm waking, I can feel myself waking, but I haven't woken up completely. In other words, what you're saying is that when you wake up and realize what's been done to you, you want to beat the hell out of everybody who's kept you down."

"Exactly."

"I understand it in principle, but . . ."

Another month passed, and then another. We continued to immerse ourselves in his obsession. He began reporting bouts of insomnia, crying jags late at night, more fits of temper at himself. I could tell that the long-repressed feelings were coming nearer to the surface, feelings that had formerly gotten acted out in his various passive–aggressive ways. Now the acting out behavior had lost its luster and the feelings were breaking through. I could sense that he was hearing what I had to say. He had begun to come on time for his sessions and to pay me on time and to speak to me with trust, as one talks to an ally. Finally, the day came when I knew that he had reached the turning point.

"I saw Louisa yesterday."

"What happened?"

"The usual. I said 'hello,' and she just looked at me and walked away."

"Then what?"

"I was angry at myself all afternoon, then last night I started feeling angry at my mother and I called her up."

"You did?"

"I told her *she* was asinine. 'Don't ever call me asinine again,' I told her. Now I feel guilty. She and my father have been acting nicer lately. In many ways I'm their most successful child. I make the most money, and unlike Burt and Mary I've never had any problem with drugs. Now that I'm the most successful, they want to be friends and pretend nothing ever happened."

"How do you feel?"

"Mixed. So is this the goal of therapy? To get people angry at their parents and blame them?"

"No. The goal is to get you in touch with all your feelings and help you work through them one by one. In doing that, you'll get in touch with feelings about your parents. But that's not the same thing as blaming them. We understand that they also had parents, and their parents had parents, and the chain of twisted communications may be endless. It's not a matter of blame. It's a matter that you're breaking the chain and asserting yourself with them, and they may now break the chain and go back to their parents, or if their parents are dead then they can go into therapy. If you don't let go of the anger and work through it, you end up taking it out on yourself or on others for the rest of your life."

He thought about what I said for a while. Then he replied. "I don't want to do that. I think I'll call my mother again tonight. Maybe I'll call her again tomorrow night. Maybe I'll call my father, too. Maybe I'll call them both every night for the next year. Maybe that's what I'll do."

He left the session with a grin.

He came back the next session and reported expressing anger at both his mother and father and enjoying it. He understood that this was a temporary ritual of passage that would enable him to come to peace with his parents as well as with himself. It was the dawning of a beginning of a new attitude toward them and toward himself.

Meanwhile, several months passed in which there was not a mention of Louisa. I wondered whether he had forgotten her or whether he was just reluctant to bring her up, fearing my disappointment. Eventually I brought her up.

"Seen Louisa lately?"

"Louisa? Who's that?" he quipped. "Yeah, I saw her. No big deal. I saw her today, as a matter of fact, and I thought to myself that she was really quite ordinary looking. She was quite common. She was with a friend and she had that same smile on her face that I used to think was so intriguing but today I thought it was a forced smile, and her body language seemed rather uptight, the way she kept folding her arms. I'm lucky I didn't get involved with her. She's a jerk."

"A jerk?" Both he and I knew this was the word he most often hurled at himself.

"That's right. A jerk. If you want to know the truth, I despise her. She can go to hell. And so can you."

"Me?"

"Yes, you."

"Why me?"

"Because you let me go on and on about her. I'm really angry at you for that. I really am. Why didn't you stop it sooner? I'm really pissed about that. I'm paying you hundreds of dollars a month, and you let me just waste it. What do you care, as long as you get your pay."

"Oh really?" My tone of voice was solemn, but inside I was feeling happy for him. I knew he was on the right track now. "Tell me about it," I said.

He did.

CHAPTER 6

The Sad Dancer

Multiple Techniques with a Suicidal Multiple Personality

First there was the suicidal urge. She would come in and sit on the floor and she would say, "I'm afraid."

I asked, "Of what?"

She said, "Of life. I'm afraid of life."

And she had slash marks all up and down her forearms and that made me feel afraid as well, and I said, "We have to talk." And I used a paradoxical Gestalt approach, joking with her, "If you kill yourself, I won't be your friend anymore." It made her laugh and conveyed the message—in an indirect and nonthreatening way—that I cared about her and that we had an attachment that was valuable. Suicide is always the result of a frustrating attachment, so I wanted to emphasize the blossoming nonfrustrating attachment she had with me.

Then she came in with her paintings and I sat on the floor with her (to build our attachment) and used expressive therapy techniques, helping her to talk about her feelings by talking about her paintings. Then she came in with her poems and I helped her to talk about her feelings by talking about her poems.

Then she came in hearing voices, shuddering, whimpering, swaying to and fro, and I used Gestalt techniques to help her say what the voices in her head were saying. And then I used expressive techniques to get her to vent the feelings that were overwhelming her and jamming up her system. I had her kick down and hit down on the couch with her feet and fists as she screamed at her mother, father, and people in her life. When she asked if I understood her pain, I mirrored her by letting her know I too had suffered greatly in my childhood. When she had trouble verbalizing her terrifying rage at her parents, I joined her anger, grabbing a tennis racket and exclaiming that I was so angry at her parents I would express the anger for her.

"Fuck all of you for abusing Jennifer the way you have!" I shouted, smacking the pillow a few times. "I hate you! I hate you! I hate you!" I realized that it was not only Jennifer's parents I hated at this moment, but my own and all abusive parents everywhere. It did not really matter where the hate was coming from, only that I was able to model to her that it was okay to have anger at parents and to give words to it.

I handed her the tennis racket and she stood squeamishly eyeing the pillow as if it were a snake.

"I can't do that," she whimpered.

"How come?"

"I . . . just can't. Please don't make me do it."

"Aren't you angry at your parents?"

"Yes."

"How angry are you?"

"Very angry."

"You'll feel better if you do it."

"But I don't want to hurt them."

"You're not hurting them. That's the point of this exercise. You're only hurting a pillow." Her grasp of reality was so blurred at that point that she could not distinguish between doing something symbolically and doing it in reality. "By hitting the pillow you're preventing yourself from really hurting them or yourself."

"I know, but . . . maybe they'll find out."

"How?"

"They will. I know they will."

"Are they in the room now?"

"They might be."

"If you two jerks are in this room now, get the hell out of here. This is my office and it's private," I shouted into the air. "Now," I turned to her.

"I still can't do it."

"Give me back the racket. I'll do it for you."

I grabbed the racket but she would not let it go.

"Well?" I said.

Her face changed. A gleam hovered in her eyes. "You want me to hit the pillow? You really want me to hit the pillow?"

"That's right."

"Okay. If that's what you want."

I was amazed at how abruptly she had changed her attitude. All at once she was hitting the pillow furiously, and snarling in a deep voice I had not heard before, "Die, you motherfuckers. Die, die, die, you bastards!" She brought the racket down with two hands as I showed her, and was hitting with such force that the racket cracked after only about four hits.

She held the racket out to me and the gleam left her eyes and she peered up at me apologetically. "I'm sorry . . . I'm really sorry . . . I'll pay for it."

Jennifer, it turned out, was a multiple personality, about whom I have written more extensively elsewhere (Schoenewolf 1991b). We were still in the chaotic beginning stage of her treatment, when she decided to reveal another self to me. On that day she brought me a gift, a tulip, which signified that she had formed a positive attachment to me that might serve to give her the strength to forgo suicide and work through her feelings. Also, she sat in a chair that day, rather than on the floor. However, she was still rocking back and forth as she always did, and hugging herself.

"How are you feeling?" I asked.

"Better." She smiled weakly.

"How much better?"

"A little better."

She had just come out of a hospital, where she had gone for a few days, at my advice, to ride out what seemed to be the worst of the suicidal storm. I had visited her in the hospital in order to further strengthen our attachment, and now she had returned looking wan but calm.

As I gazed at her I thought, as I had thought so many times, that she was the saddest, most fragile, and most beautiful woman I had ever seen. At one time she had been a promising dancer in one of New York's "off-Broadway" dance troupes. Now she had descended into an emotional hell. She was sitting on the edge of the leather chair, a tall, thin woman in her late twenties with a downward gaze and a soft, halting voice and an aura that radiated vulnerability. Most everything about her looked vulnerable: the nervous blue eyes that peered intently from a pale face etched with a sprinkling of pink freckles; the dim eyebrows and lashes that were almost the same color as her skin; the long, wavy, yellow orange hair, pulled ever so tightly into a ponytail; the faded, loose-fitting jeans, designed for a man's body, that hung lifelessly from her hips.

I found myself recalling a line from a poem by Baudelaire: "What do I care if you are good? Be beautiful! and be sad!" There is nothing more compelling than a sad, beautiful woman, which is, I suppose, why so many poems, novels, and movies are made up of such heroines.

"How's the Thorazine?" I asked. The hospital had put her on medication.

"It's okay. I still feel depressed and hopeless, but the Thorazine takes the edge off of it, if you know what I mean."

"Tell me more about the depression and hopelessness."

"It's a pessimistic feeling. A doomed feeling. It's always there, really. A feeling that I'm never going to be happy . . . never going to accept myself." She pressed her palms against her temples and closed her eyes. "Now I'm hearing a voice in my head."

"What does the voice say?"

"It says . . . I could be happy if I wanted to be. . . ."

"Then you have an optimistic part of yourself?"

"Yes . . . I guess . . . I'm confused."

Since she was sitting in a chair and there was another similar chair nearby, I decided to use an empty-chair Gestalt technique. "Let's do some role-playing. Be your optimistic self. Here, sit in this chair." I pushed the empty chair closer to her. "Sit here and be your optimistic self." I wanted to have her play out her internal voices, which I thought represented her superego and her id. The voices turned out to be a little more than that. They were her superego and id *personified.*

She hesitantly arose and sat in the other chair. "You want me to be my optimistic self? And talk to my pessimistic self? Is that what you want?"

"That's right. Be your optimistic self."

For a few moments she stared at the empty chair. Then the confused and forlorn expression on her face began to fade and her entire countenance was transformed. A small gleam appeared in her eyes, a gleam I had seen there once before when she had hit the pillows and broken my tennis racket. Her cheekbones seemed to protrude more, her jaw came out, and her eyes now bore down on the empty chair. Her posture also changed: she sat back in the chair and held her head straight. Her legs were spread out rather than primly together. She stared confidently and a bit disdainfully at the empty chair and then spoke in a strident voice.

"You *could* be happy if you wanted to," she said. "All you need to do is stop feeling sorry for yourself. All you need to do is get back to work, stop moping around, stop putting yourself down all the time." She looked at me with the same disdainful expression. "Well? What now?"

"Tell her how you feel about her. Go ahead. Tell her."

"She disgusts me."

"Tell her."

"You disgust me. You have so much talent, so much potential, but you never do anything with it. I'm tired of seeing you sit around and whine about doom and gloom. . . ." She continued to lambast her pessimistic self in effigy as I looked on. I was amazed to find that she had such a strong personality inside her and amazed at the fire in her. In fact, my curiosity had been tweaked beyond restraint. I was suddenly fascinated with this optimistic self.

"So, you're Jennifer's optimistic self. All right, let's give you a name." That was something I often did when using this technique. "Let's see . . . Big Jen. . . ."

"I already have a name," she interrupted.

"You do? What is it?"

"Margaret."

"Oh, I see. Where did the name come from?"

"I've always had it. That's my name. Margaret."

She looked at me bemusedly, as one might look at an

idiot. It took me a second to rebound from the shock of the usually submissive Jennifer suddenly eyeing me in this superior manner.

"Do you mean you were named Margaret when you were born?"

"In a sense."

"It's your middle name?"

"It's Jennifer's middle name."

"Oh." I let this statement slip by, without properly analyzing its meaning. I did not want to understand. It was too uncanny. "So when you're feeling optimistic, you think of yourself as Margaret. And when you're feeling pessimistic, you think of yourself as Jennifer?"

"No, I always think of myself as Margaret."

I was beginning to have an inkling. "Always? I don't understand?"

"I know." She flashed her superior smile. "I know you don't understand."

"What do you mean?"

"I'm not Jennifer. Never have been. I'm Margaret. We're two separate people."

"Then you're saying you have two different personalities?"

"Actually, there are seven of us."

She proceeded to tell me about the seven personalities. Jennifer, whom I assumed was the core personality, and six alter-personalities—Margaret, the fireball; Jess, the sexpot; Mildred, the intellectual; Mary, the socialite; Tom, the angry boy; and Jenny, the coy innocent girl. As Margaret described all these people, I could only sit back in wonderment. This happened in the first year of my practice. I had read about multiple personalities in books, seen them in movies, but had never encountered one. Nor had I been prepared to work with one in the institute from which I had just graduated. They were rare—so rare that until the 1960s, when *Sybil* became a bestseller, hardly anyone had heard of them.

I had not wanted to believe it at first. This, I think, is universal. Anything out of the ordinary is a threat to our ego. If somebody suddenly approaches you with a gun, you do not want to believe it. If somebody gooses you while you are standing on a crowded elevator, you do not want to believe it. And if somebody suddenly tells you she is a multiple personality, you do not want to believe it. This also may explain why multiple personalities were underreported before.

Ferenczi was the first of Freud's followers to hint at them in his paper, "Confusion of Tongues between Adults and the Child" (1933), but this paper, among the last he wrote, was greeted with skepticism by Freud. Until the late 1960s, the subject of multiple personalities was considered by mainstream psychiatry and psychoanalysis as a kind of circus sideshow. Until then, only seven cases had been reported in the literature. The profession itself did not want to believe in it, and hence, it is likely that many if not most multiples were misdiagnosed as manic-depressives, schizophrenics, and paranoids. Jennifer had in fact told me of how she had tried to reveal herself to previous psychotherapists and had been met with not only disbelief but even annoyance.

My disbelief gradually changed to awe as I gazed at this entirely new creature who sat before me. This definitely was a completely different person than Jennifer, one with a different essence. Whereas Jennifer could never show any anger, Margaret seethed with anger and was proud of it. Whereas Jennifer had no confidence, Margaret seemed supremely confident (actually it was a fake confidence). Whereas Jennifer was confused and disoriented, Margaret was absolutely focused—at that moment on me. Later, after more analysis, I discovered that Margaret had identified with the aggressor, her mother, and had copied her personality and her attitude toward Jennifer (her core self).

We stared at one another for a moment, I with awe, she with a superior grin. Finally I said, "Perhaps I'd better talk with Jennifer again. Would you mind changing chairs again?"

"You're the shrink."

She shrugged, rolled back her eyes, and grudgingly changed chairs. Her eyes went sad and her brows furrowed and her arms clung to herself once more. Then her body began rocking to and fro. "I'm confused," came Jennifer's fragile voice.

"Jennifer?"

"Yes?"

"What are you confused about?"

"I'm not sure what just happened?"

"You were role-playing. I asked you to play your pessimistic and optimistic selves."

"Yes, I remember that."

"You don't remember talking to me as Margaret?"

"No . . . I don't remember anything."

"Do you know who Margaret is?"

"I hear her voice . . . in my head . . . sometimes."

"Are you aware that you have multiple personalities?"

"I don't know . . . I really don't know . . . I'm confused."

We would go on to work together for the rest of that summer and to begin the process of integrating her personalities. Working with Jennifer was a turning point in my career. I learned more from being her therapist than I have with any other patient since then. First, I learned that with multiples you had to throw the textbook out the window, because you absolutely could not be just one kind of therapist with them, practicing just one approach. You had to be prepared to use an array of techniques, maybe all of them, and new ones you had not learned yet, including, and perhaps most important, hypnosis. With Jennifer, however, I did not use formal induction as others have. Rather, I gave her commands about paying attention to the other voices inside of her and to what they were feeling. Multiples come to you already in a self-induced trance, so it is not very difficult to informally suggest things to them.

Second, I learned much more about myself as a therapist. Because she was a lovely young woman, her sadness was all the more compelling. Multiples are all con artists; they have to be in order to survive in the toxic environments from which they are reared. They use guile and seduction to win over other people, including therapists, and they are so good at it that they can even con themselves. Research shows that a vast majority of multiples report having been sexually or physically abused before the age of 3, before their egos are completely formed; hence, their ego becomes fragmented into separate personalities. Jennifer was sexually abused by her mother and physically abused by her father. She learned about guile from an early age, when her real self was obliterated and she had to erect imaginary selves to take its place.

Working with her in my first year of therapy was a baptism by fire. My countertransference feelings were as intense as they have ever been. For much of the time that I worked with her I felt as though I were in a trance myself, and I have come to recognize since then that this was partly due to her infantile need for merger with a benign mother (her mother having abandoned and abused her in infancy); this need "entranced' me and lured me into a symbiotic vortex. I had to come to grips with my own unresolved narcissism (my need to be the hero who saved the damsel in distress), and how it made me vulnerable to her and other patients. I had to learn to tolerate the way she would transfer her relationship with her mother, father, and brothers onto me, and the disturbing feelings of hopelessness, terror, or rage this induced in me. There was a time later on when I got so involved in the rescue fantasy (in part induced by her and in part coming from my own need), that I lost sight of objectivity. I had to realize my limitations as a therapist, and understand and learn to respect the power that patients can have.

Third, I learned much about psychology. After studying her seven personalities, I became convinced that personality is for the most part formed by the environment, and does not stem from genetics. Here was living proof of that. Jennifer had formed seven separate personalities, and I was able to trace each of their beginnings (except for the core personality, who was there from birth onward) to a traumatic event in her life. Each, in addition, had identified with a different person in forming her personality: Margaret, with her mother; Tom, with his father; Mildred, with an aunt; Mary, with a neighborhood girl; Jess, with a movie star; and Jenny, with another neighborhood girl. Each personality was clearly shaped by the environment. Subsequent research has convinced me that although infants may be born with varying constitutions, ranging from passive to hyperactive, these do not necessarily stem from genetic endowments (since emotional contagion can happen in the womb), and they are not the same as character. Hyperactivity may later become paranoia, obsessive-compulsion, addiction, hysteria, but also a great accomplishment. Hyperactive infants can become criminals or generals, depending on upbringing. Passivity can become passive–aggression, schizophrenia, alcoholism, or perversity, but also a great idea. Passives are just as likely to become dentists as drifters, depending on upbringing.

I also learned how Jennifer—like other dissociated types—used dissociation, disorientation, and confusion as a defense against knowing of the harsh reality of her life and becoming aware of the things her other personalities knew. She was afraid of her own sexuality, so that had been attributed to Jess; threatened by her own anger, so that was doled out to Margaret and Tom; afraid to be too intelligent so that was given to Mildred; wary of being too uppity, so that was Mary's role; afraid to be too childlike and innocent, so that was assigned to Jenny. All these parts of herself had to be split off and disowned, yet they were kept alive in these other personalities. She had only to reclaim them, through integration, to assume her full power.

I have had many realizations since that day when, unwittingly, experimentally, I had Jennifer role-play her optimistic and pessimistic selves. Sometimes an accident truly is the mother of invention. But, no matter how far I go, I will never forget the expression on her face when I asked her, "Jennifer, do you know who Margaret is?"

It was the lost, apologetic, terrified expression of someone who has just returned from a holocaust, and is at the same time eerily matter-of-fact about it. Her answer was just above a whisper: "I hear her voice in my head."

"And the other personalities—Jenny, Tom, Mildred, Jess, and the others. Do you know about them?"

"I don't know . . . I don't know . . ."

She was shaking her head, slowly, in a daze, staring at the other chair.

"Do you *want* to know?" I asked.

"No. I don't want to know. I really don't want to know." She said it quite matter-of-factly. "I don't want to know anything about other personalities."

And so the integration process started.

CHAPTER 7

The Woman Who Did Not Need Therapy

Mirroring a Particularly Resistant, Pathogenic Personality

During the course of my training I once served as a group leader at a drug rehabilitation center that I will call "Harmony House." This center, which was located in a brownstone building in lower Manhattan, was modeled loosely after the Alcoholics Anonymous program. However, instead of alcoholics, it focused on recovering drug addicts—particularly heroin users—and their families. The program was staffed mainly by ex-addicts and their relatives, although on occasion they used psychotherapy interns to run groups. At the program's core were the nightly rap groups, where three times a week former drug addicts sat in a circle talking about their days of addiction; twice a week members of their families sat in the same room talking about the problems of dealing with drug addicts.

I was in charge of running one of the groups for relatives of drug addicts, and from the beginning of my internship, I encountered friction in the form of a woman named Mabel, a mother of three addicts; specifically, she had a need to oversee, second-guess, and cast doubt upon my leadership.

"Gerry," she would say as I entered the door, in the

sweetest, most considerate tone of voice my ears had ever beheld. "I don't want to interfere with your business, but I don't think you understand the ways of Harmony House yet. Believe me, it takes a while; I was here two years before I really knew what I was doing. And that's not a put-down, so don't get insulted, okay? I'm just trying to help. You're new to all this and I just want to help you avoid the pitfalls I ran into. You don't understand drug addicts because you don't have a relative who took drugs."

"My parents were alcoholics."

"That's different. Alcohol is alcohol and drugs are drugs. Believe me I know. I had three children who became heroin addicts. Listen, don't get defensive, I'm just trying to help. Listen, why don't you just sit back a little more in the group and notice what people are saying, that's all. Until you learn the ropes."

During the middle of the evening, when we took a ten-minute break, she would take my arm and pull me aside and say in a sugary half-whisper, "Gerry, now don't take this personally, but I think it would be better if you started the second half of the session by bringing out Margaret. She needs to talk. I can tell. Believe me, when you've been here for a while, you know."

At the end of the evening she would approach me again to say, with the most caring look in her eyes, "Gerry, I don't mean to tell you what to do, but could you be a dear and make sure all the windows in the living room are closed. Last week it rained and somebody left the windows open and the carpet was soaked."

Mabel was known as one of the pillars of Harmony House. Over the years she had made herself indispensable—cleaning, cooking, organizing, painting, plastering, running errands, and overseeing everything. I imagine that must have been her role in her family; she was the one on whom everybody depended. A large, round woman who carried herself like a truck driver but had the angelic face of a church organist, she was one of those people who are convinced that she and only she knows how to keep things clean and in smooth working order, and this gave her the right to make everybody else march to her drum. And although some people at the center jokingly complained about her, calling her "Mr. Mabel," they all did as they were told. I did as I was told too at first, for she came upon you in that guileless manner with the hail-sister-well-met attitude that suggested that it was and always had been her place to sweetly order people around, no questions asked.

At first I wanted to get into her good graces. "I don't know what we'd do without you around here," I said to her with genuine admiration and affection one day. I had thought that would be what she wanted to hear, but I was wrong.

"Oh, thank you," she replied, and the smile was almost a grimace. "Listen, I've been meaning to ask you, do you think you could make the coffee tonight? Phyllis is sick."

"Oh, sure."

"That's a dear. Just fill the scooper about 80 percent. And remember to turn it off as soon as the light goes on or it will burn."

She seemed suspicious of my compliment, perhaps aware of my growing irritation with her. At the same time, she made it known not only to me but also to others that only she made judgments, only she could praise or criticize, and anybody who made any kind of judgment about her, even one of praise, was stepping out of place. She, apparently, was beyond praise or blame.

As I observed her and learned more about her, I began to realize that she was what I call a pathogenic personality. She induced or provoked emotional pathology in others, while herself remaining quite functional, quite at the top of her form. Her communication was quite toxic, replete with double-bind statements and denials. Whenever somebody starts a sentence with, "I don't want to interfere with your business" or "Now don't take this personally," they usually *do* want to interfere and they *do* want you to take it personally, only they are denying it to themselves and to you. Similarly, when somebody tells you that what she is saying is not a put-down or that she is just trying to help, she is denying that she is putting you down and is not really being so helpful as she is being bossy (and in control). All such statements put the receiver in a double bind. If you are told, "I'm not putting you down," you are placed in a no-win situation. If you believe to the contrary, that you were being put down, and you speak up about it, you may be told you are being silly or crazy or oversensitive, which will add insult to injury. If you say nothing, you will have to suppress your feelings of annoyance at being put down.

Bateson et al. (1956) studied double-bind communication, and linked it to schizophrenic family systems, noting that parents of schizophrenic children tended to communicate with them in this manner. Theodore Lidz (1965) in his famous family studies wrote of the schizophregenic mother and father who likewise communicate in twisted ways, utilizing not only double binds but a host of other bewildering methods. When a child of 2 or 3 has such a person as a parent, the child becomes confused. A pathogenic parent may, through a characterological fault in themselves, be impatient with a child, always making the child feel stupid or slow. If the child complains, the parent will say, "Oh, you're just being oversensitive again. I love you and someday you'll understand that." So the child finds his or her real feelings and perceptions constantly being invalidated and has to repress them while developing an unreal defensive posture toward the double-binding parent. "You must be right, I'm being over-sensitive, sorry." Moreover, the child has been induced to invalidate his or her own perceptions of things (and develop an inferiority complex), and to trust that the parent will later prove to have been right (continuing the double bind). Either way—whether the child gives in to or opposes the double-binding parent—the child cannot win.

Meeting Mabel got me to thinking about the subject of pathogenic personalities. There are many such people in society, I decided—people who, while consciously having the best intentions, nevertheless unconsciously cause harm to others. Some are blatantly pathogenic. Most are more subtle, dwelling quietly in the mainstream of society. Like Mabel, they may come across as confident, dominating personalities, or they may be meek and unassuming or happy-go-lucky jokesters. The thing that they all have in common is that they have an almost unshakable faith in their own goodness. This need to believe in their own goodness, their own rightness, their own cause, is their own peculiar kind of narcissism; indeed, it becomes the very foundation upon which their very identity rests. Try to take away this aura of goodness, and you will encounter the rage underneath. That is why hardly anybody ever tries it.

I am not talking about any particular diagnostic type here, such a sociopathic or narcissistic or borderline. Rather, I am describing a certain defensive operation that may be a feature of any of several types. At the core of this operation is projective identification. Pathogenic personalities invariably deny ego-dystonic aspects of their selves and project them onto an external object. This object is then identified as the possessor of that which they deny. They then treat this object as if it has the problem or conflict that they deny in themselves. By treating the object—often a small child—as if he or she had this problem, the child, or sometimes husband or wife (or sometimes therapist or patient), eventually develops this very problem. The child develops the pathology that the pathogenic personality fears developing; the former must sacrifice his well-being so that the latter can retain the illusion of well-being.

A father may have an obsession for neatness, which defends against the fear of soiling. Within himself is a conflict between his ego ideal, which demands perfect neatness, and the id, which wants dearly to soil, with very little ego to mediate between the two. The ego ideal wins this battle. The id impulses are repressed, denied, and projected. His son is seen as embodying "the soiling" personality. The father, hence, takes charge of the son's potty training, but during the training he conveys to the boy that he (the son) is hopeless and deficient, and that he will be a soiler despite all the father's teaching. The boy fulfills this destiny and becomes a soiler. The father has managed to externalize the conflict inside of him, and his punishing superego now has an external object on which to inflict the punishment. The son develops the pathology that the father is defending against within himself.

A mother is overprotective with her daughter. She is hysterical and phobic. She denies her aggression and projects it onto the external world. She expects the external world to aggress against her and feels inadequate about dealing with that aggression, since she is not in touch with her own aggression or its related assertiveness. She then projects the feelings of inadequacy onto her daughter and overprotects her. She fears that the aggression of the world (which through projection she exaggerates) will impinge on her daughter. By overprotecting her daughter, she prevents the daughter from developing the very ego skills that would allow her to handle aggression—

her own and the world's. Hence the daughter develops a form of psychopathology.

A carpenter treats his younger assistant as though he cannot do anything right. Every time the assistant tries to knock a nail into a board or screw in a bolt, the carpenter sneers, grabs the hammer or screw-driver, and says, "Let me do it. You're never going to do it right." Again, the carpenter is projectively identifying his assistant as incompetent—this being an aspect of himself that he is denying, externalizing, and overcompensating for in this manner. Over time, the assistant will make more and more mistakes, justifying the carpenter's low opinion of him.

In all three cases, the pathogenic personalities think they are being a good parent or boss, treating their children or assistant with concern. Their ego-ideal prevents them from seeing that they are behaving in such a way as to displace anger and engender psychopathology. Hence such situations can rarely ever be resolved.

We are talking about emotionally disturbed individuals who have little inkling of their disturbance. Often such individuals are devoutly religious or politically correct. If such an individual reads a piece such as this one, he or she will probably quickly dismiss it as "too analytic" or "mother-bashing" or "too intellectual" or "too sexist." Such individuals do not believe in delving too deeply into things. In fact, oftentimes such people are in positions of authority—they may be priests or politicians or even psychotherapists. There are many psychotherapists today who subscribe to the currently trendy notion that parents are not responsible for the psychopathology of their children; rather, it is a matter of a "bad fit" between a child and its parents. Both the child and the parents, by this way of thinking, are co-responsible for what develops. This trend, in my opinion, is one of the most destructive in the

field of psychology. In traveling to other cultures where
childrearing is given more emphasis and social problems
are at a minimum—such as Japan and Europe—and
speaking with psychologists there, I found that they were
saddened but not surprised by this trend. "American
psychologists have found a way to rationalize their neglect
of taking responsibility for childrearing," one said.

Pathogenic personalities can come from a variety of
backgrounds. Often they come from dysfunctional families in which they played a heroic role that could never be
questioned. For example, an older sibling may be assigned
the role of caring for younger siblings, and along with that
role she may be given the message that she is and always
will be the mature one, the one who knows best, and the
one who is always right. The youngest in such a family
may be assigned the role of scapegoat; she may be given
the message that she is always wrong, stupid, bad. When
these children become adults, the youngest will be the one
who will have the most motivation to change. She will be
the one who goes into therapy. She will have no difficulty
in shucking off her role. The oldest, however, will cherish
her role as the mature, good, caregiver, and will want to
maintain that identity all her life. Even though she may
have contributed greatly to her youngest sister's pathology, she will never admit it. Like her parents, with whom
she identifies, she will say that the youngest sister is
neurotic, oversensitive, wayward. The youngest sister will
thus be branded, dismissed, no longer listened to. Only the
oldest sister's opinions will count.

Whatever their background, a mythology develops with
regard to their role in the family, as well as to their future
role in society. They are good, noble, right, and they
cannot be questioned. If other siblings question them, they
are made aware of their mistake. If schoolmates question

them, they too must be quickly given the message. Later, when they get married, their spouse must never question them. No, their mythological role was not designated by a Roman or Greek diety—not by Jupiter or Pan or Ares or Mars. But it was designated by someone almost as high up—the omniscient and omnipotent goddess of early childhood: Mom.

I did not know if Mabel had indeed sprung from such soil. But it did seem that her role at the drug rehabilitation center had become mythological. Mabel could do just about anything she wanted and nobody questioned it. In her zealousness she constantly made mistakes, sometimes glaring ones: she would order far too much food for a picnic, spending money from a budget that was already strained, then take the considerable leftovers home with her; break dishes in her eagerness to clean them; put misinformation into her monthly newsletter out of a need to believe and write about things she thought would happen. Many new people came to the center to try out one of the groups, only to be intimidated and offended by her. The turnover was quite high. But the old guard, the small cluster of members who had been attending for years, was firmly behind Mabel and gladly served as her *selfobjects.*

Even when it came out in the weekly groups that she had three children who had become heroin addicts, she was still not questioned. The prevailing opinion—which was the one she had herself proffered—was that her children had become addicts because they had a disease. This disease had come down on them like some plague from nowhere and had nothing to do with how they were brought up.

The night I first heard about it, I could not help but feel curious. "You have three kids who are junkies?" I repeated.

"Were," she corrected me. "They've all gone through recovery now."

"That's good. How old are they?"

"They're all grown-up now. And they're all in methadone programs."

"Great."

"I don't know why God decided to test me, but I guess he had his reasons," she said, slowly shaking her head from side to side. "I guess we all have our burdens in life, and mine happens to be three kids who became junkies." Her head bent forward and her eyes gazed to the left with a great deal of woe. "I used to think it was my fault. I mean, those kids were incredible at trying to lay guilt trips on me. But, thank God, I came to Harmony House and finally realized that my kids simply have a disease. It's nobody's fault. Thank God I'm not putting myself down anymore." Then she turned to me and said, "Why do you ask?"

"Just wondering."

"Don't wonder so much, Gerry. You do far too much wondering, if you ask me. All of you shrinks do far too much wondering and not enough listening."

She got a big laugh from her followers, and the subject was changed.

I knew from talking privately with others that not everybody believed that drug addiction was strictly a disease. Some, like me, believed that environmental factors contributed to the formation of an addictive personality. They understood, as I did, that it was not God who had turned her children into addicts. If she had treated her children the way she had treated us—doing everything for them, totally indulging them, gratifying their every needs (thus cultivating dependency and keeping their egos weakened and unable to tolerate frustration and make long-term commitments), while at the same time subtly crushing their spirits by continually putting them into double binds, this was sure to have helped to make them addicts. Yet, even though many understood this in general, nobody ever said anything about her. The mythology simply could not be questioned.

However, her relationship with me became more and more irritating. The longer I stayed, the more threatening I was to her. I was becoming known as "the bright young psychology student" and people, especially the newcomers who had not yet been ensnared by her, were expressing admiration for me. She seemed to step up the pace of her interference with my activities.

"Gerry," she would say as soon as I walked in, "can we talk? Listen, I didn't want to say anything, but last week after the meeting I found that the guys in your group left all their dirty coffee cups on the counter. . . ."

"Gerry," she would say during the breaks, "excuse me. I don't want to butt in, but I noticed in the group you were letting the men talk more than the women. . . ."

"Gerry," she would say after the meetings, "I just want to tell you something for your own good. Now don't take this the wrong way, but some of the old-timers have been complaining about your manner."

This last comment was the match that lighted the fire. "Who complained?"

"I'm not at liberty to say. Now don't get upset. They don't mean anything by it. We've all been here for a long time. I'm just trying to be a friend to you, you know?"

"Right. I know."

I went home and paced my apartment in a huff. I had thought that I understood her and that she would not be able to get to me. But she had, and I was furious. Who did she think she was, sitting in judgment of me and everybody when she herself had raised three junkies? It was time, I thought, for her comeuppance. I went back two nights later like a loaded gun, ready to go off. I made sure she and I were in the same group. When she brought up her children and started bemoaning the burden they had caused her, I quickly interrupted.

"You know, Mabel, a few days ago you were good enough to tell me some things about my personality that you thought were preventing me from being as effective as I could be, so now, if it's all right with you, I'd like to do you the same favor. Frankly, I've experienced you as being quite an enraging and confusing person at times."

"Enraging?" she muttered. She could not fathom it. "Really?"

"Yes, enraging, and confusing. You are constantly putting me into double binds, saying things to me like, "Now don't be offended," or "Now don't take this personally"—and everytime you do this it's presumptuous. You are presuming to know what I'm going to feel, and it prevents me from just being whoever I am. As I said, it's enraging and confusing. And you are always doing everything yourself and not letting anybody else do anything and then complaining that nobody else ever does anything. And if you did this to your children, then it would be bound to have an effect on them. I mean, all you ever do is talk about what a burden your children are on you, and I imagine they are, but how do you think they got that way? Who trained them? Instead of coming here and complaining about your kids, have you ever thought about going into family therapy with them and trying to straighten out the errant communication, or of going into therapy yourself?"

Mabel looked at me with utter incredulity. "Go ahead," she said in an even tone. "I want to hear this. You've been dying to say this to me. Go ahead, say it all."

"I'm finished."

"You're finished? Are you sure?"

"Yes." I had begun to feel a little sick, knowing that I had allowed myself to be provoked, sensing I had fallen for the trap.

She smiled at me as one smiles at a wayward child. "You're funny. You know that? You're really funny. I'd laugh, but actually it's not funny. It's sad. It's sad that there are people like you in the world. I've been busting my butt trying to help you since you came here, trying to show you the ropes because I know what it feels like to be a newcomer. I've been going out of my way to try to help you feel comfortable, and this is what I get. I could tell from the beginning that you weren't really a Harmony House–type person, that you'd never really understand addiction or the family life of addicts. But I thought, 'Maybe I'm wrong. Maybe he'll grow.'

"I figured you'd probably say something like this to me sooner or later. I had the feeling about you from the beginning. You want to know what I think? I think you hate your own mother, and so you want to find reasons to hate me. Shame on you. Shame. You've come here to my place, to my Harmony House, and tried to humiliate me here in front of my friends. Shame." The smile left her face and her voice broke and tears appeared on her cheeks. "Everybody knows how much I've done for Harmony House, and everybody knows how much I've done for my kids. How dare you throw my kids up to me like this! How dare you! I don't know how they do it in whatever therapeutic institute you come from, but here at Harmony House we don't attack each other. Thank God I've been here long enough and gotten the support I have, or your attack might have destroyed me. I won't take that rap anymore. I did the best I could for my kids, and if they have a disease that's not my fault. And for your information, I don't need therapy. How dare you come here and insult me. How dare you attack me this way! Shame! Shame!"

"Mabel's right. You're got your nerve," another member said.

"I feel like kicking you out of here right now," another said.

"No, let him stay," another said. "He's still new. He'll find out."

"How are you doing, Mabel?" another cooed. "Are you all right?"

"Yeah, yeah. I'm all right." She sobbed bravely. "Thanks. I'll be fine. Just forget about it. He didn't mean it."

"The only person who needs therapy in this group is you," another put in. "That's a therapist for you," he continued, chuckling. "Always telling people they need therapy."

For some reason, the whole group fell into hysterical laughter.

In the days that followed Mabel and everybody else seemed to forget what was said that night. In fact, for several weeks, neither Mabel nor anybody else said much of anything to me other than to formally greet me. Then one night Mabel alluded to it obliquely while sliding back into her familiar routine. I came into the door and she waved cheerily at me just as she always did, bounding toward me with her angelic smile. "I was hoping you'd come early tonight. I had something I wanted to discuss. Listen . . ." She took my arm into hers and glided me off to the side. "I need to ask you a favor."

"Yes."

"Now, don't get defensive."

"I'm not defensive," I said, feeling suddenly defensive.

"It's not a big deal. I'm not trying to tell you how to run the group."

"All right."

"You're new here, that's why I'm pulling you aside like this."

"I've been here almost a year."

"I know, I know. I'm not trying to boss you. I have no reason to boss you."

"All right, Mabel. What is it."

"I mean that. You have to trust me. Stop overanalyzing things, okay." She patted me on the back of the head, as if I were her little boy. "Okay?'

"Okay."

"You overanalyze too much. I'm just telling you that as a friend."

"Okay."

I wanted to say something to defend myself, but I realized that it would have been a futile exercise and even worse than futile: self-defeating. Anything that I or anyone else said that did not support her belief system was simply ignored. It was as though she had her own personal ozone layer that automatically blocked out all "ultraviolet" comments.

She beamed at me and I obligingly smiled back. We stood there, smile to smile, and I could see that her smile was only a mask, with telltale rays of anxiety flashing from the whites of her eyes. I could also see a desperate conviction in the wrinkles around the eyes, as if she were saying, "This is me, do you see? This is me, I really am a wonderful, kind, giving, hard-working person with only the best intentions! Please, please, please, don't question me!" In that moment I could see how terribly frightened she was of me or of anybody like me who might dismantle the tenuous construction of her idealized self-image, and I also had a brief fantasy about how it must have been for her children—how they, too, had been required to never challenge this ideal image of herself and never confront the double binds and invalidations she threw at them, unconsciously. There really had been no way out for them accept to act out, letting her continue to play the saint, while they were relegated to playing the sinners. Then I had another even-briefer fantasy of her as a terrified little girl, compensating for her terror through the erection of this brittle narcissistic shell. She really was fragile, I suddenly realized. Like Humpty-Dumpty, she could easily fall and crack. But inside her was no yolk, only a void.

We looked at each other and then I felt the anger reside and saw myself putting my arms around her to give her a hug. All at once a wave of affection, a resigned and begrudging kind of love slithered through my body and I found myself embracing the desperate, lonely little girl inside of her who needed everybody's absolute and unblinking faith and obedience. I understood, in that moment, something that I was going to need to understand with my private patients from then on. I could not yet put it into words, but it had something to do with avoiding power struggles, refraining from giving interpretations when interpretations were useless, and learning to tune in to the "patient's" unconscious. I believe it was also at that moment that I used my first paradoxical intervention.

"What's the favor, Mabel?" I said, taking her arm in mine and clasping it tightly.

"Well, it's just that I've noticed—and other people have remarked about this, too—when you end the meetings you tend to do so a little too quickly, not giving people time to adjust. I just thought . . ."

"Mabel, what a wonderful suggestion. You always come up with wonderful suggestions," I said, clasping her arm even tighter and looking smilingly into her eyes. I felt love, hate, sympathy, and fear, all at the same time, and I wanted her to see it in my eyes. I wanted her to feel the full intensity of what she had induced in me. "Listen, I've been meaning to ask you if you'd mind coming in early from now on so that you and I can discuss things. I have so much to learn from you. Would it be too much to ask? Just an hour or so early—what do you think?"

"Oh, sure," she said. Her smile was suspicious. Her eyes fell away from mine for a second—something that had never happened before.

"And by the way. I want to apologize for what I said the other day, about your needing to go into therapy. I shouldn't have said that. You're a pillar of Harmony House. You're fine." I was not lying exactly. I really believed that Harmony House was her therapy, and always would be. "Please forgive me," I added.

"It was nothing," she said, waving me off, but her eyes dropped again.

"So you'll come early next Tuesday?"

"I'll try."

"Oh, please. I need your help. I really do. You know everything about this place. Please."

She tried to disengage her arm from mine, but I clung to it a little bit longer. She looked up as if to ask what was going on. I smiled blissfully—as she had previously smiled at me—with perhaps a tinge of anger underneath. Finally I let go and we shook hands and I made it a point to kiss her on the cheek, which made her pull away. As I walked off, I turned and saw that she was still looking at me suspiciously.

She did not come early on Tuesday, and when she did come in, unusually late, she did not have time for me. Some new members had gathered near the door and she took it upon herself to orient them—although that was normally somebody else's job. Once or twice I sought her

out to ask her advice but she waved me away and said,
"You know the ropes now."

During the remaining two months of my internship I did
not have any more trouble with her.

CHAPTER 8

The Couple Who Fell in Hate

Paradoxical Behavioral Techniques in Couples Therapy

It did not take them too long to fall in hate. The day after they were married it had already begun. She had hoped that marriage would finally get from him the commitment and passion she wanted. He had hoped that marriage would finally shut her up. It did neither.

They were like many couples nowadays who form what I call a passive-aggressive coupling. He was passive-aggressive, and she was aggressive-passive. In other words, he behaved passively in a way that induced aggression, and she behaved aggressively in a way that induced passivity. Instead of becoming loving mates, they ended up in a stalemate. Mornel (1979) wrote a book about this syndrome, giving it a humorous title, *Passive Men and Wild Women.*

Terry came to me for individual therapy, but after her marriage she spent her sessions complaining almost exclusively about her husband. She was a pretty woman in her thirties, well read, sensitive, but terrified of men. Her father had been a passive man who had provided for the family but had been emotionally absent. Her mother had been a competitive woman who derided her daughter's looks and turned her into a tomboy. My patient needed her husband's sexual approval and he would not give it to her.

Her husband, Tom, a devout Quaker, appeared to be the perfect mate. In many ways he was very attentive to her. He cooked wonderful meals, did windows, was handy around the house, and never lost his temper. He believed he was a spiritual and concerned person. Twice a day he meditated, and often he went away on meditation retreats. Yet, despite all this, my patient continually felt furious toward him, finding herself saying sarcastic things to him in front of people at parties, causing people to wonder (sometimes aloud) how come this nice guy put up with this monstrous wife.

"I don't understand it," she moaned during her sessions. "He seems to bring out the monster in me. He's so good, I can't stand it. He keeps wanting me to do meditation with him, implying that if I just calmed down, things would be all right. He thinks everything's my fault—that I'm hysterical, and that's why we have problems. If I yell at him, he just looks at me with a sad expression, like he's thinking, 'Why, God, have I been burdened with such a witch?' When I complain that he isn't interested in sex, he says maybe he would be if I weren't so sarcastic to him! You see, that's what he always does; he always passes the buck to me. I can't stand him! I want to strangle him! I want him to disappear! I hate him! He disgusts me!"

Tom was disowning his own aggression and projecting it onto the wife: "I don't hate her. I'm not a hateful person. It is *she* who is the hateful person." However, he passive-aggressively provoked hateful feelings in her by frustrating her. This was all the more galling because he was doing that while appearing to be Mr. Nice Guy. He had this ideal image—the image of the good Quaker—that had to be lived up to all costs. He could not harbor any hateful thoughts and had to always be right and good. He was sure he had only love for his wife, and if she would only calm down, everything would be fine. His family had been one in which no cross word was ever spoken and in which only the purest sentiments were allowed. In such an atmosphere, real feelings and thoughts must be repressed, and aggression can only be leaked out passive-aggressively.

Meanwhile, Terry was disowning her aggressive-passivity. Consciously she thought that by aggressing against her husband she could browbeat him into submission, but unconsciously she wanted to push him further away into his passivity so that she could have an excuse for her self-righteous indignation and volatile behavior. She had been reared in a volatile house, in which the alcoholic parents had continually fought, as she put it, "like a cat and a dog." She always had the impression that her father, a politician, married and had children only because it was politically expedient to do so.

Just as her own mother had ranted and raved at her passive father until he would finally explode and then retreat further into passivity (and be doubly cold to my patient), now she would rage at her husband until he would do likewise. Then they would have a fight in which they shoved and slapped one another, called each other names, and sometimes threw nearby objects. Afterward there would be a period of calm, and he would meditate longer than usual and promise to try to make love to her.

"That's all he does is promise," she would mutter after these fights. "He comes up to me with this humble look, brings me food, drinks, acts real nice. But it's all an act. It doesn't mean anything. I hate him!"

"What would you like me to say to you?" I asked.

"I don't know."

"Do you want to make the marriage work?"

"No. I don't want it to work. Why should I want it to work?"

"Do you want to separate?"

"I don't know. No, I'm too afraid to separate."

She was caught up in this conflict, paralyzed by it. She did not want to save the marriage and she did not want to end it. Yet she was too upset to do anything other than complain. She was in continual crisis and continual rage. I could see that the two of them were enmeshed in a conundrum. She would rage at him until she pushed him over the brink. He would lose his temper and feel remorse. Then he would apologize and promise things. She would feel better for a day or two, but remain cynical. Soon he would resent having been browbeaten into an apology and would become passively-aggressive again, ignoring her in bed, in the kitchen, in the garden, making his meditation his lover.

One day she came in and said, "It's over. I'm finished with him. I've had it. We just had another fight and it's over."

"What happened?"

"Oh, he was in his room meditating and I just couldn't stand it anymore, and I went in and I just slapped him. I was really surprised. I just walked up to him and slapped him." She had a happy, incredulous tone in her voice.

"What did he do then?"

"He got up and shoved me against the wall."

"Then what?"

"We started throwing things, calling each other names. The usual. It's over. I can't stand him. I just want out."

I had decided by then that the only way to work with her was to use a behavioral approach that dealt with her by dealing with her husband. He was her life; her self-esteem and equilibrium depended on how their relationship was doing and on whether or not he desired her. She reminded me of Maggie in Tennessee Williams's *Cat on a Hot Tin Roof.* She was too upset to listen to any kind of analysis or to be objective.

So I gave her assignments designed to change the nature

of their relationship. These were behavioral games, based partly on the Erickson model (see Haley 1973), which I had extended (Schoenewolf 1995). I understood that sexuality was the biggest problem area, and I started with that. I told her to play a little game with her husband. Some night when they were lying in bed, or when he was watching television, she was to unzip his trousers and arouse him. However, upon getting him excited she was to drop everything and exclaim, "I'm bored with this." Then she was to turn away and pretend to go to sleep. If he tried to continue the sex by mounting her, she was to reject him. If he complained about her teasing, she was to acknowledge that she was indeed teasing him.

She protested that she did not want to approach him for sex, even if it was to tease him, and was skeptical that such a plan would work. I had to keep proposing this plan and variations of it for several sessions, using a kind of informal induction to persuade her that it would be a different way of expressing her aggression, a way that might bring closeness rather than distance, or at the least might be a step toward resolution. "You'll be mirroring your husband's sexual rejection of you. That will help him see what he has been doing and it will relieve you of some of your anger." I went over this game with her several times, emphasizing to her that it was important that she be ready for an angry reaction from him, and that as soon as she saw any sign of anger, she should drop the game and use the occasion to have a discussion of their relationship.

Was I tampering? Was I playing with fire? These were questions I asked myself. However, I did not feel that anything I suggested could result in worsening a situation that was already near the breaking point. I also knew that if things continued to escalate, somebody might be more drastically injured. Sometimes therapists must intrude, like referees, when fighters are fighting dirty. Sometimes they must experiment like physicians trying to find the right "tranquilizer." It was better to do something than to sit back and be passive, like her husband.

But why use a "game"? One of the first principles of therapy is that you have to meet the patient on the patient's level. As I said, it was impossible to talk to her, just as it is impossible to talk to anybody who is involved in a feud or brawl. Since they were involved on a game-playing level, I decided a game would be the antidote to it. Of course, a therapist has to be careful in using any kind of active technique, especially one that may backfire. I recognized that in this instance there was a possibility that her husband might become violent. No matter how well you may think you know a person or a couple, you can never predict anything with certainty. As a safeguard, I kept repeating my instructions to her, particularly the instruction to cease and desist as soon as she saw that she had engendered his anger. The purpose was to get him in touch with the anger he was denying and acting out by sexually rejecting her, not to get him to act out that anger in a violent way. I spent a considerable amount of time orienting her toward anticipating this possibility.

There is an art to hating, and that art has to do with hating in such a way as to bring about closeness rather than distance, with mending rather than destroying. Since they were a couple who were in hate, you had to use that hate in order to get them out of hate, but use it in a constructive way. In order to immunize patients against a disease, a physician often injects them with a small amount of the infectious agent from that disease (Spotnitz 1976), and the antidote to a toxin may be another toxin, as when vinegar is used as an antidote to ammonia poisoning. Similarly, as Winnicott (1949) pointed out, sometimes people need hate in order to hate. If you try to love someone who is bent on hating you, they will hate you even more. If you hate them back, but hate them with the intent of getting them to see their own hate and thereby bring understanding and closeness, this may be the proper antidote to their hate.

Their relationship had become a ritual rather than a real thing, a compulsive war to prove each other's badness. The ritual served secondary gratifications having to do with needs that had not been met in their childhoods and developmental phases that had not been successfully traversed. He needed to assuage guilt and feel powerful by inducing her to become monstrous toward him and showing that he could endure it. She needed to vent rage and feel self-righteous in order to compensate for feelings of low self-esteem. Each needed to prove himself or herself right and the other wrong. Their very selves depended on it. Their egos were both so underdeveloped, that their superegos had to do battle, one ego-ideal against another. Neither could mirror the other's ego-ideal, hence the battle raged on interminably.

The games I devised had an element of risk, and I was willing to take responsibility for that risk.

So I persisted and finally she agreed to do it. The next session she said, "I tried your game but it didn't work."

"What happened?"

"Oh, I started giving him a blow-job and then said, 'This is boring,' and turned away like you said, but nothing happened."

"He didn't complain?"

"No, he just kept reading his book."

"Then you'll have to keep doing it until he complains."

"This is silly."

"I know, it's terribly silly."

"I feel childish, like I'm playing a childish game."

"It *is* a childish game, but your relationship is childish, so a childish game is what works best with children; anyway, it's being played with a therapeutic aim."

Next week she came back and said, "I did the tease again and we had a fight. Is that what was supposed to happen? I teased him and he asked me why I was doing it and I told him that was what he did to me and then he shoved me out of bed. I had to sleep in the other room. Next morning he said we needed to talk."

"That sounds good. What did he say the next morning?"

"Oh, it was so stupid. He said that the reason he didn't want to have sex with me was because I didn't respect him. That's what he always says."

"Do you respect him?"

"No."

"Then he's right."

"How can I respect such a wimp?"

"Maybe you can't."

"I can't. I really can't."

"So do you want to try to try to make it work?"

"No."

"Do you want to separate?"

"Maybe."

I could see a slight change in the balance of her conflict.

At this point I again suggested, as I had before, that she and Tom seek out a couples therapist. She protested that Tom would be resistant and complained that she was the one who always had to initiate everything. After a few weeks of this she finally found a therapist who was in the neighborhood.

She returned from the first session with this therapist doubly upset. "We went to see the couples therapist and now I'm even more confused about everything and even more disgusted. I think I'm just going to quit therapy altogether."

"Why?"

"Well, when she heard that I had slapped Tom she gave

me this long lecture about physical violence. Then she said she wouldn't work with me unless I had medication, and referred me to this psychiatrist. Then she said Tom had to work with a male therapist and I had to go into individual therapy with her. When I told her I already had a therapist, she said I shouldn't be seeing a male therapist and that you didn't understand me and weren't helping me. Neither Tom nor I got a word in edgewise. Nothing is changed. In fact, it's much worse.''

It took me a while to calm her down. The next day I located a woman colleague who agreed to take the case. I felt it was important that the couples therapist be a woman, to balance things out gender-wise, but a different kind of woman. My colleague began working with Tom and Terry the next week, providing a calm, nonjudgmental space in which they could disengage and mediate their dispute. After the first session, I asked Terry how it had gone, and she said, ''Better. She's much better.'' She said she had decided she wanted to get a divorce, and I joined her, saying, ''Yes, I think that's the best thing.''

Throughout this phase of my therapy with her, I had to use eclectic techniques. There was absolutely no chance to do any psychoanalytic work. At times I felt more like a social worker than a psychotherapist. Yet, that is what was called for so that is what I did. During the period in which she was frustrated by her sexual relationship, I used an erotic game to try to diffuse the situation and bring some kind of resolution. When more resolution had come, I advised couples therapy. When the first couples therapist exacerbated rather than helped matters, I secured another therapist and (with the permission of my patient) prepped her for her task. When my patient at last decided she absolutely wanted a divorce, I joined her, knowing that her ego was not strong enough to go through the vicissitudes of such a proceeding without being bolstered.

Indeed, it became clear to me that Terry's childhood had been so dysfunctional and had left her with such a weakened ego that she was virtually flooded with anxiety and depression and was out of control the entire period of her therapy, which lasted several years. Her mother and sister had both been that way as well—histrionic to a borderline degree. The only way to do therapy with her was to act temporarily as her strong alter ego and wait for the erotic emotional storms to subside. Freud (1905) once called the hysterical attack "an equivalent to coitus" and had he been alive now he might have been talking about Terry. Her fits were obviously compensating for sexual frustration and could have been seen not only as sexual provocations but also as rapes.

Afterward, when the divorce was final and she had had a chance to start a new life, she felt calmer, happier, and kinder. At that point, she was able to do the work of analysis.

"I guess you see me as a monster," she said one day.

"Why would I see you that way?"

"I don't know. Maybe that's how I see myself. I wasn't very empathic toward Tom."

"You think not?"

"Maybe it was my fault that the relationship didn't work."

"How so?"

"I really didn't respect him. I didn't respect my father. I didn't respect my brothers. I don't think I've ever respected any man. I was trying to get Tom to give me love, but I was doing it the same way my mother used to do it with my father. By yelling at him and putting him down."

"You think if you had respected him, the marriage would have worked out?"

"No. It might have been better. But he had his problems too, and he's even more resistant to therapy than I am."

"That's true."

"For some reason, I'm feeling emotional."

"How come?"

"I guess I'm feeling emotional about . . . you. But I don't know if I'm supposed to have these kinds of feelings about my therapist."

"On the contrary, you should have whatever feelings are inside you and verbalize them. It's important for the therapy."

"I guess I feel grateful. I guess I feel . . . respect for you. Yes, that's it. I think you're the first man I've ever really respected."

"How does it feel?"

"Good. Embarrassing. A little scary."

"Respect is *very* scary. Especially when you've never gotten it."

"It is. It really is."

CHAPTER 9

Ariel in the Bluebonnets

Eclectic Techniques for Generation X

It is something about being theatrical. "You're just being theatrical," or "Stop being so theatrical," or "Do you always have to be so theatrical?" She has not really heard it, only felt it. The words have become an enormous sting deep inside some dark, unprotected chamber of her heart. She sees the knife on the kitchen counter and picks it up without thinking about anything in particular. The knife lies in her hand. She smiles.

Now she sits in the middle of the kitchen floor looking at the knife. Now she flips it from one hand to the other. Now she tosses it into the air and catches it. Now she smiles at it. Now she slides it lightly across the palm of her hand, drawing a tiny drop of blood.

"Ariel, give me the knife."

"No." She smiles at the knife, serenely.

He reaches out to take it. She stabs at his hand.

"Ariel, why are you doing this?"

"You said I was theatrical. So I'm being theatrical."

"Give me the knife."

"You know, John, sometimes you're so idiotic. Especially when you try to act like a male authority figure."

"You didn't think I was so idiotic this morning."

"I was just acting, dear. I'm always acting. You should know that."

"Give me the knife."

"No."

He leaps upon her, pins her to the floor, and wrenches the knife free from her hand. She bites his arm, ripping his skin with her teeth. He gasps and jerks his arm away, gawking at it. "You bitch!" he mutters, giving her shoulders a shake. She laughs and grins and says, "Oh, what a strong, clever man you are. Aren't you a strong, clever man?"

Waving her away, he raises himself up, tosses the knife into his shirt pocket, and sits down in his easy chair to resume reading a magazine.

"That's right, read your magazine. Find out what today's politically correct opinions are so you can add them to your repertoire."

"Whatever you say," he mumbles.

"Are you a feminist man, dear? Sure you are. Do you support our tropical forests? Of course you do. Are you for civil rights? Naturally you are."

"Whatever you say."

" 'Whatever you say.' That's very clear, just keep answering 'Whatever you say.' That's so very clever." She puts her mouth to his ear as if to kiss it, and then hisses, "Whatever you say!"

He bats at her with the back of his hand. "It isn't amusing."

"You forgot to say, 'Whatever you say.' "

"Right."

"No, no, no, no. You're supposed to say, 'Whatever you say.' You're forgetting your lines. Here, I'll help you." She takes his nose in one hand and yanks down his jaw with the other. "Now say it: 'Whatever you say.' "

"You're sick. You need a shrink."

"Whatever you say, dear."

"You're a sick woman."

"You *make* me *sick. You make me want to throw up. I can't stand it! I really can't stand it! I'm going to kill myself right now. I'm going to throw myself out of the window." She rushes to the window, stands on tiptoes, and stares down at the street. "I'm going to kill the next person who walks by. I'm going to throw myself on the next person who walks by and then vomit all over him." She begins to climb the sill, and the man groans and rises reluctantly from the chair. Without a word, routinely, he pulls her out of the window and shuts it.*

"Idiot, idiot, idiot," she shrieks, pummeling him with both fists. She whirls away and lunges to the bathroom, slamming the door behind her. "You're nothing but an idiot and that's all you'll ever be!" she shrieks through the door. "You think you know everything and in fact you're an idiot!" Trembling, she opens the medicine cabinet so hard that several vials clatter to the floor. She finds a razor and takes out the blade, smiling.

"Ariel," he says, standing outside the door.

"Come in, dear."

When he enters she has already slashed her wrist. She drops the razor onto the floor and sits on the toilet seat, holding her arm in one hand as though it were not a part of her. Blood oozes toward her elbow.

Now she smiles with curiosity at the wound. Now she smiles at him. Now her head falls back and she snickers, shutting her eyes and shaking her head in disbelief. Now she points at him with a finger that curls from her bleeding arm.

"You should see your face," she says. "You have such an idiotic look on your face. Like like some boy who just

got his pee-pee caught in the refrigerator door. What a
wonderfully idiotic look." She laughs and laughs. "You
look just like a silly, confused boy."
  "I'll get the bandages," he says.

Borderline personalities are often barometers of their era;
due to a lack of genuine attachment and a heightened
sensitivity to people, they respond most strongly to life's
ebb and flow—particularly to all that is pathogenic. With
no real center, no real self to call their own, they are
constantly in terror of being contaminated, not by disease
but by rage—theirs and others'. They are driven personalities who quite often burn themselves out like moths
circling a lightbulb, hurrying through life, taking the
measure of each instant, lashing out at all they feel and see,
reflecting the sickness of their immediate world and of the
times.
  Ariel was such a person. As soon as she entered my
office I could feel the strong current that emanated from
her. "I had to speak to somebody," she said with a
desperate calm. "I'm afraid I'm going to fall into the abyss.
A few days ago I had one of my rages and I tried to kill
myself. It wasn't the first time." She spoke in a peculiar,
lazy way with a slight Spanish accent, her dark, intelligent
pupils flashing at me as she spoke. Her voice and manner
were calm but, at the same time, she was agitatedly
buttoning and unbuttoning the neck of her blouse. "I'm
really quite afraid. In fact, I'm terrified."
  She had not so much walked as glided into my office,
light of foot and wan of expression, a world-weary waif,
yet with a body ego ruled by angst. Her jeans were
wrinkled, her cotton smock was blotched with the stains
of oil paint, and her hair hung from her head in disarrayed
strands that partly hid her eyes; yet there was something

clear and sharp in the midst of this chaos. She was like someone out of a Botticelli painting, with pale skin, a Roman nose, and large, dark eyes that peered luminously from underneath the wavy locks; yet her brooding mouth, cynically furrowed brows, and Birkenstock sandals bore the distinct stamp of postmodern adolescence.

I asked her what she meant by rages.

"Rages? Ah, yes . . ." Without further ado she began to talk in a rambling manner. She sat forward the whole time, her long, delicate neck slightly arched, her eyes gazing probingly and yearningly into my eyes, the palms of her hands rubbing slowly against her thighs. Her voice conveyed a deep exhaustion with life—as if at the age of 24 she had already seen it all—and at the same time her manner exuded an animated, childlike fascination with her own words.

"What do I mean by rages? I scream and throw things and become abusive toward whoever's around. Sometimes I abuse myself. If there's a knife or razor around, I'll grab it and try to cut myself. When I'm in one of my rages I lose control completely. I can't stop myself and nobody else can stop me. A rage can last for an hour or for days.

"Sometimes it feels as if nobody is taking my feelings seriously. My boyfriend, John, for instance. He doesn't take my feelings seriously. No matter what I say to him, he just doesn't get it. He thinks it's just a game I'm playing, and it's not. He's amazing. It's really amazing how shallow he is. Yet he thinks he's profound. He writes these screenplays that are so facile and shallow and he fancies that he's so clever, and he's not. Sometimes he infuriates me, and I don't know why.

"A few days ago I was at his apartment and suddenly I just couldn't stand him anymore. I don't know why. And then I felt it happening and I couldn't stop it." She related the details of the rage that had led to her cutting her arm, still speaking in her lazy, indifferent manner. She talked about taunting John, about wanting to knock him down from his perch of imperturbability. "John doesn't know how to deal with me. He tries to act macho. He tries to be fatherly and give me lectures. That's exactly what my father used to do. John thinks I should go back to Chile, but I don't want to. If I went back, I'd have to be around my family.

"I suppose you'll want to know about my family background. Therapists always want to know about that. I think it's all quite boring, but if you insist I'll tell you. Do you want to hear about it? Of course you do. I come from a well-to-do Chilean family. My father is in the Chilean government; he's a cabinet minister, sort of like the Secretary of the Treasury. My mother is a college professor of literature. She has two Ph.D.'s and my father also has two Ph.D.'s. My parents are fiends about education. They're obsessed with it. My mother's never stopped taking classes since I've known her. She's now working on her third Ph.D. She's British and Jewish, and my father is Chilean. You're probably wondering about my accent. It's because my mother is British; I spoke English before I spoke Spanish.

"I'm the eldest of four children. I have two brothers and one sister, but I'm closest with my sister Florence, who's the next oldest. She's the only person in the world I really love. She's amazing. She knows so much for her age, much more than I did at her age.

"I went to all the best schools in Chile. When I was 11 my whole family had to move to England, because there was a coup and my father had to flee the country. I attended a private school on the outskirts of London for two years. That was one of the darkest periods of my life. We lived in a suburb of London and it felt as though we had been sent to Siberia. I felt like a nun. We were the only Chileans in the neighborhood, and we were so isolated. It was really dreary.

"I came to America right after I graduated from college. At first I had a scholarship to the Art Student's League, but then I lost it because I wasn't producing enough art. John wants me to go back to Chile; he thinks—and my parents also think—that my problems with painting and with everything else are because of New York. New York, they say, is making me crazy. But I don't want to be around my mother and father. I think they make me crazy. My mother gets into her moods. You never know how she's going to be from day to day. Sometimes she's sweet and sometimes she's a monster. When she's sweet she does anything for me, idealizes me, thinks I'm a genius. But when she's in her monster mood she thinks I'm bad and that everything's my fault. Does that make sense? She was always this way. I remember as a small child she would sometimes rush into my room at two or three o'clock in the morning, wake me up, and yell at me and tell me how rotten I was and how everything was my fault. I was always terrified of her.

"My father always sides with my mother, no matter how irrational she is. If I go to him to complain about my mother, he'll give me a long lecture. He wears me down. He's like John, he's great with words, with ideas, with logic. No matter what I say, he'll always have an answer. After a while I just fall silent. Does that make sense?

"When I was 15, I stopped talking to both of them. I stopped talking to everybody and I went through an anorexic period. I stopped eating and my weight fell to an impossible level. I think I weighed about 79 pounds or something ridiculous. That's when they first sent me to see a therapist. I didn't mind. All my friends were going to therapists. Everybody in Chile goes to therapists. Seriously, it's amazing. Therapy is even more popular there than in New York, if you can believe that.

"I've had three therapists, all of them women. That's why I came to see you this time; I wanted to try a man. All my therapists became mother figures, and then they'd start becoming too attached and too interested in me—intrusive, as they say. After a while I couldn't stand them and had to get away from them. The last one wasn't so bad, the one I went to in New York. She's the one who first told me I was a borderline personality. She tried to explain it to me but I'm not sure I understood. She said I depersonalize. That I separate myself from my feelings. Does that make sense?

"Most of the time I feel as though I'm standing outside myself looking at myself. I'm amazed at the things I say and do. Even when I'm in the midst of one of my rages, there's a part of me standing back and watching it all, wondering what's going to happen next. I never know what I'm going to feel from day to day. I never know what I'm going to feel in the next instant.

"I think the main reason I came to you is that my friend Beatrice was recently admitted to Bellevue. She took an overdose of sleeping pills, and I had to take her to Bellevue myself. The doctors diagnosed her as a borderline personality with depressive features. They asked me about my relationship with her and I told them how she and I had taken a two-month car trip around the United States without once ever stopping to spend the night anywhere. The doctors said our relationship was a 'folie à deux.' Have you heard of that? They said we were both crazy in the same way.

"Beatrice is my best friend. She's more than a friend; we sometimes feel we're just alike, twins. Once we walked from one end of Manhattan to the other—from Battery Park to Inwood without ever stopping to rest. I've always liked to walk. I never stay still. When I was in Chile, I often walked from one end of Santiago to the other and back. Beatrice and I like to walk together. We also paint and write together. She's a genius. She makes up words. We have our own special language and nonverbal communication system. When we're with other people, she'll give me a certain look or smile, or I'll say a certain nonsense word, and the two of us will start to giggle. Everybody thinks we're crazy. Sometimes they get annoyed.

"Since we got back to New York we've been writing a book together. It's a novel about our adventures this summer, when we drove around the United States. So far it's over 500 pages long. It's a very intense experience, writing this novel. It's not like doing a painting. Everybody who's reading the book thinks it's amazing. We're trying to do something nobody's done before. A kind of stream of consciousness. It appears chaotic, haphazard even, but in fact it's profound. At least most people think so. It reflects the confusion of the times.

"I can't stand most of the fiction being written nowadays, or most of the art that's being done. It's all so shallow, so facile, like John's screenplays. I can't stand minimalism. It's stupid, don't you think?—a clever trick to cover lack of depth or talent. The characterizations in today's fiction are trite and the perspective topical. It's the same thing with movies. American movies are particularly bad. I can't stand them. They have the most amazingly stupid plots, and the actors all behave like teenagers, even if they're old. Nobody seems capable of transcending the moment. Beatrice and I are trying to do something that transcends the moment. When we finish our book I'll bring it in for you to see.

"I didn't know I was going to chatter like this. I thought I'd have trouble opening up to a man, and yet here I've chatted away for an hour. So tell me: What do you think?"

She began formal treatment the next day. It was a dreary, rainy day in the beginning of October, and she arrived nearly an hour early. When I opened the door to the waiting area she jumped right up and glided into my office, beaming. She had on black tights and a short, plaid skirt that showed off and accentuated her long, girlish legs. "Where shall I sit?"

"Do you want to lie on the couch?"

"I don't mind. It'll probably be relaxing."

She plopped on the couch and lay back dutifully. "What shall I talk about?" She tugged at her skirt, raising it to her knees.

"Whatever thoughts come into your head."

"No thoughts are coming into my head."

"Everyone has three or four thoughts a second," I said, giving her my standard line.

"Really? I'll bet you just made that up."

"No, it's true. They've done research. People tend to have three or four thought impulses a second."

"How can they tell that?"

"By measuring brain-wave activity."

"Oh."

"Anyway, I wonder why you aren't able to become aware of one of your three or four thoughts a second?"

"I don't know." She pulled her skirt past her knees. "Perhaps something's inhibiting me. It suddenly occurs to me that I don't know you. You're a complete stranger."

"A stranger?"

"A stranger, and a man."

"What if I am?"

"I don't know if you'll be able to understand me. Most men don't understand the least thing about women. They think they do, but they don't. Like John, for instance. He writes these screenplays about women, and he fancies that he understands them. He thinks of himself as a man who knows women and can write about them with feeling. But he doesn't know them at all. I think that's one of the things that depresses me most about New York. You have all these little boys running around thinking they're men and that they understand women, and they don't."

I found myself feeling bemused. She had such a fresh-faced, pubescent appearance, with dark, adorable eyes. This was in stark contrast to the bitter things that came out of her mouth. One would expect such pronouncements from, say, an aging female alcoholic, but from her they sounded strange. In addition, these bitter words were delivered in this offhanded, somewhat sulky and seductive manner, and she would turn from the couch in between phrases to smirk at me and check out my response, as though each phrase were some test. I found myself having impulses of wanting to laugh at her or tousle her hair or kiss her. I knew that these impulses were being induced by her manner, and knew also that she probably induced them in other men as well.

"So men are all little boys who can't understand women?" I said. "How about me? Is there any chance I'll be able to understand you?"

"You're a shrink," she quickly replied. Then she changed the subject, something she would do often. "Actually, I feel safe with you. You seem different from other men. I feel safe here in this office." She looked around. "I wish I could stay here forever!"

"What would you do if you stayed here?"

"I'd lie around, read, paint. Nothing special. Just ordinary things."

"What would I do with my other patients?"

"You could still see them. I'd stay out of the way."

"That's decent of you."

"I thought so."

"Where would you sleep?"

"On the couch, I guess."

"So, should I ask you to move in?"

"Maybe." She turned to flash a conspiratorial smile. "That might be nice."

"And what would our relationship be like after you move in?"

"I don't know. This is embarrassing." She raised her skirt again, then lowered it. "Do you always ask such embarrassing questions?"

"I try to."

In fact, I did not always ask such embarrassing questions. I was being rather confrontational with her because of the kinds of feelings she was arousing in me and what I knew this to foretell about her pattern with me and with others. She had started off by being quite seductive, and I wanted to explore her fantasies about me as a way of heading off her acting out these fantasies. With certain patients one does not touch such fantasies for years, but with borderlines, one confronts them right away. "So how would it be if you moved in?" I persisted.

"I'd always feel safe."

"Always?"

"Well, at least until I got into one of my rages. Then maybe you wouldn't want me around anymore. Or maybe I'd think you were weak or an idiot and leave you. Usually after a while I can't stand the men I'm seeing and I leave them. Usually after I have sex with them I can't stand them anymore. When I first meet them I can't wait to have sex with them, but then right afterward I can't stand them. I guess that's what would happen if I moved in with you. I'd want to have sex with you right away and then I wouldn't be able to stand you anymore.''

"And then you wouldn't feel safe anymore."

"Probably not."

"And then you'd leave."

"Right."

"Doesn't sound too promising."

"I guess not." She flashed another conspiratorial smile.

Two days later I picked up the telephone and put it to my ear. A singular, urgent, yet offhanded voice throbbed from the receiver. It was Ariel's.

"I'm sorry to bother you, but . . . is it possible to see you today? I'm scared. I'm scared of how I'm feeling. I'm scared I'm going to . . . do something . . . to myself or to somebody else."

"You'd better come in."

She came right away and sat outside on the street for several hours. I could see her through the window, sitting on the railing of my building, reading a book, shading her eyes from the sun. At about ten minutes before her appointment she rang the buzzer and came inside to the waiting room. When I opened the door, she scurried in like a furtive rabbit, not looking at me, her face glum and her body rather stiff. Her hair was in disarray and matted from perspiration. She wore no makeup and had on a wrinkled blouse and baggy jeans. She did not lie on the couch, but sat on it, her knees primly together, her hands folded, gazing off, away from me.

"What is it?"

She took a breath, let it out, then began to talk in a frenzied clip, like some wind-up doll that had been over-wound.

"I went to see Beatrice yesterday morning and it depressed me. She's suicidal and she's making me feel suicidal. Whenever she feels suicidal I also feel suicidal. That's the way it always is. And whenever I get this way I think I don't want to be in New York. All day today I've been thinking about how much I can't stand it here. I can't stand being alive. I can't stand my apartment. I can't stand John. I can't stand my parents. I can't stand anybody. I'm terribly, terribly agitated. I feel like I'm going to fall apart. I'm so terrified that I'm going to fall into some abyss of rage and forgetfulness and never come out.

"After I left Bellevue I started walking and I didn't know where I was going. I just kept walking and then I got to this bridge and somebody told me it was the Brooklyn Bridge and I walked over it and kept walking. I had no idea of where I was going, do you know what I mean? And then after a few hours—or was it a few days?—I saw the ocean in front of me like some vast, billowing beast of freedom, like some carefree, mindless beast of freedom, and I was standing on the boardwalk of Coney Island, just standing there for a long time gazing at the ocean as it licked at the shore. Then I walked along the boardwalk as far as I could, passing Brighton Beach and then I walked across a long, long bridge that seemed to go on forever and I finally came to a place called Jacob Riis Park, and there were a lot of naked gay men lying around grinning at me and then I was on Rockaway Beach and I walked all the way along the beach until I saw a sign that said "Airport." I walked and walked, following these signs until I got close enough to see the planes landing. By then it was night and I sat in the airport and did not move from my seat until dawn. I really did not move at all; it was as if something were holding me in my seat, some invisible force. I just sat there in the terminal watching the planes come in and go out, and especially the noses of the planes, and the little men, the little pilots in the windows above the noses, which looked like giant eyes looking at you, or like small eyes inside of big eyes, as the huge nose of the plane came toward me. All night long the noses came toward the terminal, right up against the window where I was sitting, right into my face, and the pilots seemed to be looking at me out of the eyes of the plane, and I just gazed at them and I wasn't thinking anything at all. Then the sun came up and I began to walk again and eventually I found my way back to Manhattan. When I got home Beatrice called me from the hospital and I felt sick. I wanted to just go out on the street and kill somebody. I don't know why. Or kill myself. Does that make sense? Then I phoned you.

"The only place I feel safe is in your office." She glanced up at me. She was sitting forward from the couch. "I don't know what to do. I feel so terrified of everything. I don't trust myself. I don't trust being alone with myself. When I feel like this, I'm afraid . . . I'm afraid . . . What should I do? Please, tell me what should I do?"

In the yellow lamp light of my office, in the still of the evening, her arms wrapped around her thin, pale body, she looked so utterly lonely, miserable, and vulnerable.

Originally the term *borderline* was used to designate a patient who was almost, but not quite, schizophrenic—that is, on the borderline of schizophrenia. Ferenczi (1933) seemed to allude to borderlines when he wrote about "the almost hallucinatory repetitions of traumatic experiences" that began to occur with frequency in his daily practice, by patients who had been severely traumatized in early childhood, many of them sexually. These patients had developed "splits in their personalities" which he called a form of "atomization." Helene Deutsch (1942) shed light on the "as if" quality of some of her more depersonalized patients, resembling today's borderlines, whose "relationship to the outside world and to their own ego" appeared "impoverished or absent." She showed how the lack of ego integration, splitting, and depersonalization leads to the development of an "as if" or false personality.

Fenichel (1945) described patients with impulse neuroses who are intolerant of tensions. "Whatever they need, they must attain immediately. The infant, as long as he acts according to the pleasure principle, tries to discharge tension immediately, and experiences any excitement as 'trauma,' which is answered by uncoordinated discharge movements" (p. 367). Overcoming this state, according to Fenichel, requires the capacity to change uncoordinated discharge movements into purposeful actions, and the ability to delay gratification. Such patients act instead of thinking, and their actions are not directed toward achieving goals but getting rid of tension. "Any tension is felt as hunger was felt as an infant, that is, as a threat to their very existence." Impulse neurotics typically try to rid themselves of tension through temper tantrums and through running away. The act of running represents a fleeing from a supposed danger or temptation, or a running toward reassurance—toward a "helping oral mother." While the runner usually projects the danger onto the environment, the real danger from which he or she wants to flee is internal depression, rage, and guilt.

Melanie Klein (1946) expanded Freud's definition of splitting, underscoring the importance of splitting as a defense mechanism of the ego at regressed levels of behavior in schizoid patients. Rapaport and colleagues (1946), through psychological testing, isolated a group of "preschizophrenic" patients who revealed a predominance of primary process (childlike) thinking and a marked ego weakness in comparison with typical neurotic patients and yet did not demonstrate true symptoms of psychosis. Hoch and Palatin (1949) described what they called "pseudoneurotic schizophrenia," which is very similar to preschizophrenia. Erik Erikson (1950) focused on identity diffusion in certain patients with borderline symptoms. Such individuals are unable to form a single cohesive sense of themselves, and their identity is confused and fragmented. They do not know who they are or where they belong, and they usually experience chronic, subjective feelings of emptiness, a contradictory self-perception, and contradictory perceptions of others. Gregory Zilboorg (1941) wrote of "ambulatory schizophrenia," denoting a type of patient who had symptoms of schizophrenic withdrawal, yet nevertheless function in the world—and are in fact ambulatory.

From the 1950s on, more and more was written about the borderline personality, and it began to evolve as a basic character type in its own right. W. R. D. Fairbairn (1951) furthered the study of the object relations (their relations with themselves and others) of borderline schizoid and hysterical personalities. Michael Balint (1968) described the basic fault (or fixation) that caused borderlines to be susceptible to "malignant regression." James Masterson (1981) noted that borderlines suffered from an "abandonment depression," and developed a clearly defined therapy technique for working with them, combining supportive and interpretative techniques. However, it was Otto Kernberg (1975, 1985) who defined and described the borderline character most concisely and thoroughly.

Kernberg observed that borderline personalities at first appear to be typical neurotics, but upon closer inspection they are found to have an underlying borderline personality organization. The most prominent borderline symptoms are (1) a high amount of free-floating anxiety; (2) a tendency toward polysymptomatic neuroses, including combinations of phobias, obsessive thoughts, hysterical

physical symptoms, dissociative reactions, hypochon-
driasis, and paranoia; (3) polymorphous-perverse sexuality; (4) a prepsychotic personality structure involving
paranoid, schizoid, or hypomanic (wild) trends; (5) impulse and addiction problems; and (6) a tendency toward
chaos and chaotic behavior.

Kernberg portrays borderlines as having weak egos, so
that they cannot tolerate anxiety, control their impulses,
or develop subliminatory channels (such as practicing an
art). Their fundamental problem is an excess of aggression,
which spills out on others or on themselves. They tend to
think in a primary process, childlike way and are highly
ambivalent, due to the defense mechanism of splitting.
Most were severely traumatized as children by parents or
caregivers who denied doing so; hence, these children
grow up with confused perceptions of reality and wide
fluctuations of mood. While normal people may, during
fits of rage, tend to vilify spouses, parents, or bosses as
all-bad, borderlines tend to be in a chronic state of enra-
gement and to chronically view most people as all-bad,
and feel justified in viciously attacking them; they have
never integrated (accepted) the good and bad in themselves and are unable to make such a fine distinction in
judging others.

Borderlines, according to Kernberg, do not have the
capacity for mature love or empathy; instead, they tend to
establish demanding, clinging relationships to idealized
individuals, to whom they turn for gratification and pro-
tection, or they devalue and persecute people in order to
obtain a feeling of magical power. They often sexualize
their relationships; there is a "flight to promiscuity"
among both male and female borderlines, which is an
attempt to assuage anger, deny envy of the opposite sex,
and avoid guilt feelings. Both Masterson and Kernberg
agree that the primary fixation of borderlines is some-

where between the oral and anal stages—the age at which children discover the differences in the sexes and at which they are toilet trained. It is at this stage of development that a normal child achieves ego integration and forms a cohesive self-perception.

Kernberg found that female borderlines tend to be particularly angry at men. This is because during the early oral phase, before the age of 2, they are severely frustrated by their mothers or other primary caregivers, leaving them with a desperate need for primary love and caring. Later, during the oedipal phase, they are particularly intense and seductive toward their fathers, attempting to substitute genital gratification for the gratification of their frustrated oral-dependent needs. Often, fathers react rejectingly or inappropriately to these heightened, childlike oedipal overtures from their daughters. Usually they are weak men who present a united front with their wives, even if their wives are obviously inadequate. Since the father is their last resort, and he too rejects them, these girls retain as adults a deep bitterness toward men.

Ariel certainly seemed to have many borderline symptoms. She had an excess of aggression (her rages) that got taken out on others or on herself. She spoke of herself as "always acting," and of standing outside herself, corresponding to the depersonalization and dissociation described by Deutsch in her paper about the "as if" personality, and by Erikson in his exposition about identity diffusion. She was constantly on the run, like Fenichel's impulse neurotic, and lacked the capacity to change uncoordinated discharge movements into purposeful actions. She had Masterson's abandonment depression (felt abandoned by her mother), and she fit Kernberg's descriptive analysis, presenting much free-floating anxiety, a combination of neurotic symptoms (anorexia, obsessive trends, dissociative states, depression, and paranoia), pro-

miscuity, and impulsiveness. She was highly ambivalent
and prone to splitting, vacillating between the poles of
love and hate in her attitude toward her parents and all
those around her, alternately idealizing and devaluing
people, including her lovers and therapists.

My work with Ariel was still in its beginning stage, yet
such was her impact on me that I already felt I had known
her for a long time. She was both strange and familiar, new
and old, innocent and cynical. She had burst into my life
like some cry in the middle of the night, a person whose
many gifts had been waylaid and damaged by the severe
frustrations of her childhood environment. I was convinced that with her gifts she could have been whatever
she wanted, achieved whatever she desired. Under different circumstances, she and I might have been friends.
Instead she was caught up in the web of her borderline
process, unable to relate to me or anybody: a beautiful,
exotic bird with magnificent wings who could not fly.

November was dismal that year, with many rainy days and
many other days when gray clouds squatted down over
the city and would not go away. Ariel came to her sessions
and sometimes she would glance out of the window at the
rain and the clouds, but she did not linger on them. The
days moved on and the rain fell in small, pesty droplets
tapping on the windows, and she would lie there anxiously playing with her ring, glancing toward but not
directly at the windows as she talked on in her ancient
adolescent voice.

For a while she came in every day in a manicky mood,
rambling nonstop about her usual pet subjects. She might
start with her parents, then the men in her life (usually
more than one), then comparing Chilean culture to Amer-

ican culture ("Americans are so stupid. Their idea of a good movie is *Star Wars,* a fairy tale for kids!"). Sometimes she would compare Chilean women with American women, but eventually she would always get around to her favorite subject—a comparison of Chilean and American men.

"I hate New York men," she would say, lying languorously on the couch, sliding her gold sapphire ring on and off the fingers of her left hand. "I really do. I can't deal with them. I can't figure them out. They're amazing. They think they're great, and they're not. I was so disappointed when I came here. I thought American men were going to be like the men in the movies, like John Wayne and Humphrey Bogart. Where are they? They don't know how to flirt, how to relate to women. Chilean men know how to flirt. They're the best flirts.

"There are three kinds of American men, basically. One type is beautiful but gay. This type is very soft and in touch with his feelings and cultured, but afraid of women. Another type is neuter and goofy, you know what I mean? I don't understand this type. Like little boys who haven't grown up. Most American men are like that. The third kind if sexy, but the few sexy men are always neurotic or weird in some way, addicted to drugs, angry at women, afraid of commitment."

"What category do I fit into?" I asked.

She turned to flash a coy smile. "You? You're a therapist. I don't think about you that way. And besides, you're too old."

The next day she told me a long story about how a young man had been following her around and knocked on her door and tried to convince her to marry him and have his babies. As she was telling me this story I noticed that she was lifting her hips up and down in a sexual motion. Every now and then she would glance around from the couch and smile invitingly. Her sexuality was permeating the room.

"What are you doing?" I said at one point.

"I don't understand."

"You keep moving your hips up and down."

"Do I?"

"Yes. And smiling at me, and buckling and unbuckling your belt. What does it all mean?"

"Do you think I'm trying to seduce you? That's interesting." She grinned and looked pleased.

"Are you?"

"You're very clever." She turned her head all the way around to smile at me, bestowing the kind of pretty grin that Marie Antoinette might have offered to a clever, yet inferior servant. "You've found me out. Yes, I've been teasing you. I'm always teasing men. I've done it for years, ever since I was 17, ever since I came out of my anorexic stage. I never just relate to one man. I'm always having a multitude of romantic relationships at the same time, but I only sleep with one or two men at a time. I mean, I can never remember a period of time when I wasn't sleeping with somebody. I've slept with thousands of men. But mostly I just tease them. Some men get really angry about it, they take it so seriously. Especially American men. Most men aren't as clever as you. They have these huge male egos, and they don't understand it's just a game. Sorry if I offended you."

Sexuality, I realized, was for her like a recreational drug, a temporary balm to divert and quiet the demons inside. Her teasing was an attempt to get rid of the demons, to frustrate others and inject others with the rage that consumed her. Yet she was not without a conscience, and her periods of teasing and rage were often followed by periods of remorse and depression.

"I'm in my nun period," she said on one of these days. "When I get like this I don't feel anything. Nobody understands me. You don't understand me."

She had come in and sat up on the couch, her long wavy hair, as usual, uncombed and hanging haphazardly from her temples, with one wayward strand dangling between her eyes, across her nose, and around her mouth, which she made no effort to lift. She was wearing an old denim jacket from which a button was missing, and she kept it on and sat with her hands in her pockets.

"What don't I understand?" I asked.

"You don't understand how desperate my situation is. My parents have been paying for my therapy and pretty soon they won't have any more money. There's a horrible inflation in Chile. All my friends are telling me not to come back to Chile, it's terrible there. I don't know what I'll do if my parents can't send me money. I don't have working papers. I'm feeling paralyzed. Depersonalized. Like I'm never here. Like I'm always acting. Even when I'm having sex I'm acting. Nobody really knows me. You don't know me."

"What don't we know?"

"You don't know what a monster I really am." She glanced up to probe my eyes. "Things are desperate with me. I don't have any money and I don't want to keep asking my parents for money. I don't know if you understand how desperate things are."

"What do you want me to do?"

"I don't know. You're the therapist. Lock me up somewhere."

"Should I put you in an institution?"

"Maybe." She did not seem enthusiastic about that idea.

"Can your parents afford to pay for a private institution?"

"No. I don't want to depend on them."

"Could you ask them for help?"

"I don't want to ask them."

"Then I'd have to put you in a public hospital, like Bellevue."

"Not Bellevue. That's where Beatrice went. It was horrible, I would never want to go there."

"I might be able to get you in someplace else."

"I don't think I could stand a hospital."

"I could refer you to a psychiatrist I know, and he might prescribe some medication."

"I don't like the idea of taking medication."

She would come in frantic, wanting me to "do something," but invariably negated every idea I offered. She did not want to talk about it, she wanted action. "You're the therapist," she would say, meaning I was supposed to know what she needed and just do it. I should just take charge of her like a big safe Daddy-bear and hold her and feed her day and night until she found her lost soul. This is what she missed as a small child, this was where she was blocked, this was what she needed now in order to move on.

Indeed, what she was asking for was not so farfetched. Other therapists had taken patients into their homes, with varying success. Donald Winnicott (1949) described how he and his wife unofficially adopted a sociopathic orphan boy who became so difficult that Winnicott confessed having impulses of "every now and again murdering him." John Rosen (1962) wrote of how he involved himself physically with some schizophrenic patients, letting them live in his home, allowing them to regress to an infantile level of functioning, then feeding, bathing, holding, and cuddling them in order to soothe and heal the psychic wounds of childhood. At the same time he would make "deep id interpretations" explaining to them what had happened in their childhood and how it had affected them, talking with them in the "language of the unconscious." Rosen demonstrated dramatic results using this technique, but critics have contended that these results only occurred during regressed states and question whether the improvements were lasting. Since Rosen did not do follow-ups on these patients, there is no way of knowing whether Rosen or the critics are right. Innovative therapists are like shamans or artists; they venture out of the conventional paths and sometimes achieve spectacular results and sometimes fail just as spectacularly.

For obvious reasons this was not feasible in Ariel's case. First, and most important, it would have been a violation of professional ethics to become personally involved with her. But even if it had not been a violation, I was a bachelor at the time, and it would not have been practical to have a single woman patient living with me, nor would it have sat well with the woman I was seeing. Second, I was not sure I would be able to withstand the rages that I knew would get taken out on me, my apartment, and my neighbors, if she had moved in with me. Third, I was not at all convinced this intervention would be best for her, because while it might have gratified her immediate need for a holding environment, it might also have led to destructive complications.

I also knew that her complaints about nothing happening, about not understanding that she was a monster, were a warning and a provocation. In effect, she was telling me to do something *or else*. At times when her rage flared up she felt envious of all those around her who were calm, particularly men, and wanted to stir them up and infest them with her rage and induce them into helping her re-create the traumatic events of her childhood. I was aware, too, that her rages had immediate reasons; she usually came in feeling frantic and monstrous after talking with her parents on the telephone.

I took a middle course, letting her know I appreciated how desperate she felt, but refusing to give in to her demands to do something.

"I want you to know I do take your feelings very seriously, and I do understand your desperation and I do understand that you have a monster inside you," I told her. "It would be nice if I could come and stay with you twenty-four hours a day or if I could invite you to stay here twenty-four hours a day and be the good parent you never had. And actually there's a part of me that would like very much to do just that." She smiled and I nodded. "Yes, I know, that's what the little girl inside you wants. But that's neither practical nor would it really be best for you; in fact, I'm sure it would defeat the therapy. What I think would be best is for us to continue the treatment five days a week as we are, and for you to learn to talk about your feelings. If you can't get money from your parents, and if you can't work, then we'll have to make other arrangements." I paused to let it sink in. She was quiet for a while. "What do you think?"

"I guess you're right."

She was quiet again. I sat behind her, looking at the back of her head. Her hair had fallen over the edge of the couch and dangled motionless as if each strand were in thought. "What are you thinking now?"

"About my parents."

"What about them?"

"I don't know what to tell them."

"Are things really so desperate? Have your parents really told you they can't pay for your therapy anymore?"

"No, they didn't say that. But they keep telling me to come home and I feel guilty staying here and asking them for money for therapy, especially since I seem to spend a great deal of my time in therapy talking about them. Anyway, I feel a little better now."

"How come?"

"Because I think you really *do* take me seriously. You're different than my father and John. They just look at me and shrug."

"How about lying down on the couch then?"

"All right."

She rolled onto the couch with a welcoming smile. The frantic quality was gone and her dark, intelligent eyes softened into a rueful gaze. She fell silent again.

"What are you thinking now?"

"For some reason I was thinking about my younger sister, Florence. I miss her. I miss her so much. I love her more than anybody else in the world. Even more than Beatrice. I was sort of her mother. In fact, I was more of a mother to her than my mother. She became my ally. She was so wise for her age. When my mother had her fits, Florence paid no attention to her."

"Were you the chief target of your mother's fits?"

"Yes, until my younger brother came along."

"What was it like when she had her fits?"

"It was horrible. She was like a monster."

"How old were you?"

"I think I was about 3 . . . ."

In a quiet, resigned voice, she told the story of her early childhood.

Midnight and the halls of the house are quiet and the night woods outside Ariel's bedroom window slowly come alive.

It is like nature sighing, she thinks, as she drifts in and out of sleep, like nature breathing and yawning as the world runs, blowing into the grooves and hollows of dark trees filled with water so that they call out like sad flutes, puffing on the waves of the pond so that they murmur against the shore, shaking the branches and the leaves of the trees, sending frogs out of holes, alerting the crickets so that they rattle like a thousand castanets.

Now comes another sound, a jagged noise scraping across the night, that makes Ariel turn in her bed. It is a terrible noise, a shrieking mother's voice and a rasping father's voice, rippling like uninvited guests into her sleep.

Now she opens her eyes. "Mama? Daddy?"

Now she clutches the covers up to her eyes.

Now she shuts her eyes oh so very tight and brings her left hand up to her mouth so that she can suck her thumb.

In the other room the voices are jumping up and down and talking of hate and death, and their pitch and force make the house and Ariel's room jump up and down. The inside of her body is also jumping, and outside of the black screen that covers her bedroom window the crickets are making a frightful noise and the stars seem to tremble in the sky, as if the woods were in protest and the stars were blinking in disbelief. She presses her face into the cool satin blanket, feeling sick with the sickness worse than any other, the dread of inevitable doom. From this doom she cannot run, cannot hide.

Now comes a crash as Ariel's door flies open and her room somersaults into light. She opens her eyes and everything is red and spinning. A woman stands over her, a woman who looks like her mother but is not her mother. This woman has red eyes and hundreds of teeth and hair that hangs like dark tangled vines over her ashen face, and she is smiling like a monster, smiling like she knows and hates everything about Ariel.

"You think you're a little princess, is that what it is, dear?" The monster woman's voice roars at her. "That's right, you can be calm and look sweet, because you know I'm the one who's always upset, I'm the one who's

miserable, and it's your fault." The monster stands with her hands on her hips, clad in a transparent nightgown through which Ariel can glimpse patches of breast and pubic hair.

Ariel rolls away, clamping a pillow over her head with both hands.

"Look at me when I'm talking to you!" the monster says, and she plucks up the pillow and throws it across the room. "Don't you turn away from me when I'm talking. Pardon me, have I shocked the little princess? Has Mommy shocked the sweet and so very innocent princess? Pardon me, but we know differently, don't we dear? We know you're not a princess at all, but a little monster, don't we? You're the little monster who ruined Mommy's life. Right, dear?"

Ariel gawks at this monster who calls her a monster, keeping her eyes on her, and begins to suck with more zeal on the thumb of her left hand while reaching underneath her white linen nightdress with her right hand to squeeze the tender place between her legs in a quick, desperate rhythm. Everything has gone unreal and her ego cannot grasp it. She cannot even begin to fathom what is happening, cannot in any way understand or deal with this monster who only a short time ago was the mother who was her world, the source of her every need, her first ambassador to life, whose breasts were once her breasts, whose warm milk was once her milk, whose every breath was a buoy of love and hope. She looks at this monster-mother and tries to find some trace of the real mother who was her protector but has now abandoned her. She cannot see how these two mothers can both be the same person, and she cannot put them together in her mind.

"What are you doing?" the monster asks, yanking Ariel's arm away from her mouth. "Don't suck your thumb when Mommy's talking to you. It's not polite. And

*what may I ask are you doing with your other hand?" The
blanket tumbles into the air. "Just as I thought. Bad girl.
Bad, bad girl." The monster bends the offensive hand
away and pins both arms against the headboard, leaning
her monster face very close to Ariel's. "You think you're
Daddy's little princess? Of course you do. Daddy's little
princess, prancing around the house, playing with her
little* bolsa, *right dear? Did Daddy tell you to do that? Did
he?" The monster leans even closer to Ariel, who lies
frozen and shivering against the pillow, her big brown
eyes globs of fear beneath her brown bangs. "It won't
work, dear, no matter how clever you think you are.
You're not going to get to me, and your innocent act
doesn't fool anybody."*

*Ariel begins to cry. She has fought it as long as she can,
but now her face crunches up and her mouth begins to
gasp and she lets out a shrill howl that blares out into the
caverns of the house like a siren call and then fades into
the night woods.*

*"Stop that this instant," the monster growls, shaking
Ariel. "Stop that whining. It won't work. None of your
tricks will work. I said stop crying right this instant, or
I'll give you something to really cry about. If I'm miserable then you have to be miserable too, because it's all
your fault. You brought trouble and so you must have
trouble. Misery breeds misery. Now stop it! Stop it this
instant!" She shakes Ariel so hard that Ariel thinks her
head might snap off, and then she goes numb and quiet as
a rag doll.*

*This can't be happening to me, Ariel thinks, and as the
monster continues to rage Ariel slowly floats upward, out
of her body, toward the high white ceiling. When the back
of her head grazes the ceiling she hovers there, curiously
observing the girl who was once Ariel but is now only a
mindless, spiritless, emotionless shell of a self, and she*

feels sorry for her. "Poor Ariel," she thinks. "She's so foolish and weak." And as she glides in the warm air near the ceiling, she smiles and sucks her thumb and squeezes her bolsa. *She can suck and squeeze as she pleases, and she can smile at the monster yakking away below. "Look at me, Monster, look what I'm doing. I'm doing something dirty and you can't stop me. Ha, ha, ha," she says as she floats smirkingly with one hand at her face and the other between her legs, flapping her knees to propel herself forward.*

"That's right, it's all your fault, everything's your fault," the monster goes on talking to the shell of Ariel as though it were the real Ariel. The shell of Ariel just gawks at the monster, keeping her always in view, while the real Ariel is floating near the ceiling watching it all. Outside the crickets are rattling, as if nature itself were bearing witness, and Ariel thinks, "I'm so glad this is not happening to me. I'm so glad it's happening to Ariel down there. I wish there were something I could do, but there isn't. Poor Ariel."

And then the door flies open again and knocks against the wall, and Ariel's tall, handsome Daddy is there, holding the monster by the waist. "Celia," he says, "Come to bed."

"Well, well, it's the prince himself."

"That's right. Come to bed."

"You're touching me."

"Will you come back to bed?"

"I don't care what I do. I can't stand this life. I wish I were dead. I'm going to kill myself, or maybe I'll kill you, or maybe I'll kill Ariel. How would you like to die, Ariel? Would that be pleasant?"

"Stop talking nonsense."

"Nonsense, he calls it. Nonsense. That, from Mr. Sensible himself. How are things up on Mount El Dorado, Mr.

Sensible? Just once I'd like to see him have a real feeling about me. About anything. Just once I'd like to see him take me seriously."

"I do take you seriously. Now will you please come to bed?"

"That's all you care about, your desires of an animal. What about my feelings? Do you have any concern for my feelings?"

"I do, I definitely do. Come."

"You're touching me! I said you're touching me!" The monster is screeching like a wild bird.

"The neighbors."

"To hell with the neighbors." She darts to the window, tries to open the screen and cannot. She picks up a vase, scatters the dried flowers on the rug, and flings it through the screen. "To hell with neighbors," she screeches, poking her head through the hole in the screen. "To hell with the world!"

"Celia," the father says, stepping gallantly forth.

"And to hell with husbands."

"Celia, come away from the window."

"And to hell with families." She whirls from the window and shoves the father aside. "Especially families. Do you know what families are? Families are traps. Families are wife traps. You are a wife trap," she says to the father, "And you can go to hell." She strides past him and turns to the shell of Ariel. "And you are a Mommy trap."

"Celia, stop it now."

"Go to hell."

She hurls herself out of the room. The father trails after her, and Ariel watches from the ceiling and thinks, "I love my Daddy. I love my handsome Daddy." The father closes the door, and Ariel can hear his voice and her voice bobbing and jangling down the halls and then another door closes and the voices become whispery echoes swirling about the house.

She flaps her arms and swims around in the air near the ceiling waiting for the world to settle down and the crickets to quiet and the father and mother to shut up and the light under the door to go out. She watches the shell of her self as it lies gawking expectantly at the door, and she thinks, "That wasn't my real Mommy; that was the Monster-Mommy. And my handsome Daddy came to save me. I love my Daddy." The house snuggles up into the arms of the night and Ariel glides down, flapping the air to slow her fall, and slips back into her shell. "My Daddy," she thinks, and shuts her eyes as the sounds of the woods stream through the hole the monster made in the screen and softly hum her to sleep.

Next morning the good Mommy is back again as Ariel sits in her highchair alongside her nannie, Maria, eating her cereal.

"Hurry up and finish your cereal," Maria says.

"Let her be, Maria," her mother says.

"But she's just playing with it."

"She's sculpting, Maria. She'll be a great artist some-day. Won't you my precious?" The good mother hugs Ariel and kisses her on the top of the head. "What are you making, dear?"

Ariel does not answer nor look at her mother. It makes her angry that this good mother has come back and the monster mother is gone and no word is spoken about the night before. It makes her angry that her good mother is so sweet, and she does not know why she is angry or whether she should be angry at the good mother, who is so good, and who does not seem to know the monster mother at all. So she looks down into her cereal bowl, where she has formed a replica of her Daddy's penis out of the wet flakes. Using the spoon, she builds up another layer of flakes.

"That's beautiful, whatever it is," her mother says.

"It's lovely," Maria says. "But perhaps you could take a bite of it now and then."

"Let her be, Maria. She's learning."

"Maybe so, but if she doesn't eat, she'll die with a big brain and an empty stomach."

"Don't talk like that."

"It's the God's truth. It really is. A child needs to eat, and that's the truth." Maria, who is part Mayan Indian and has dark skin and Mongoloid features, always has a look of annoyance on her face.

"You're right, Maria. You're a hundred percent right. But just let her play a while longer."

"If you say so. But a child has to eat, that's all I'm going to say. There's a time for playing and a time for eating."

"Mommy has to run to school," the mother says to Ariel. She hugs her again, splashing many wet kisses on her face. "Are you my precious angel?" she asks. Her voice is high and sweet now, nothing like the monster's. "Are you my little darling?"

Ariel is still numb from the night before and does not look up from the bowl nor respond to the kisses. She pats Daddy's penis with her spoon and studies it. Ever since her mother showed her in a picture book that Daddies have penises and Mommies do not, she has become fascinated with penises, particularly her Daddy's. She was very upset when she found out that she could not have a penis. It was like finding out that other people had three arms and she only had two. She felt cheated. Again and again, she had asked her mother when she would get her own penis, and her mother had just laughed and said that little girls did not ever get a penis, that instead they had a bolsa, *a pocket that a penis could fit into. And she asked if Daddy had a penis, and if Daddy would put his penis in her* bolsa, *and her mother laughed again and said that her* bolsa *was not for Daddy's penis, that she would have to save it for her future husband, and that her husband could put his penis in her* bolsa *and make a baby. And Ariel said she did not want to wait until she grew up, she wanted to have Daddy's penis in her* bolsa *now.*

"That's my little genius," the mother says, standing over her. "You're going to be twice as beautiful and twice as smart as Mommy when you grow up. Won't she, Maria?"

"Not unless she eats her cereal," Maria says crossly.

The mother hugs Ariel one last time, and Ariel looks up at her and is awed by her mother's beauty. She is a lovely, 24-year-old woman—the same age as the Ariel who now lies remembering her—dressed fashionably in a pink cotton summer dress that accents her thin but curvaceous figure, the bodice of which is held up only by two thin straps and is low enough to show that she wears no bra and has the small but shapely breasts admired by the educated class. Her face is innocent and shining as an angel, and her long, wavy hair gleams as it falls to her shoulders, and Ariel thinks she looks like a picture of Snow White that she has seen in a story book. She hopes she can be beautiful like her good mother when she grows up, not ugly like the monster mother, who looks like the queen in "Snow White." "Be nice to Maria today," her mother says. "I'll see you tonight." And she hurries out the door.

"Eat your cereal before it gets cold," Maria says.

Ariel smiles and pats her Daddy's penis with her spoon.

In the afternoon she plays in the backyard and waits for her Daddy to come home. She likes to play on the grass under the chinaberry tree at the edge of the yard where the trail leads into the woods. Sometimes she will run off into the woods, thinking she will keep running and find another family to live with, but Maria will always chase after her and bring her back. She likes the woods. The woods are mysterious and friendly and sweet-smelling, and there are red and blue macaws that sit high in the big-leafed trees squawking mischievously and also silly toucans that have beaks like bananas and seem to watch over her. Sometimes she will drift out of herself, especially if she is numb like she always is after one of her mother's rages, and she will fly up and hang in the air alongside one of the toucans and eat his banana-beak. After she has eaten it, the beak will slide down into her belly and grow into a yellow penis. The toucan does not mind losing a beak, for he can grow it back instantly.

She can sit on the carpet grass for hours playing with her dolls, breathing the breeze from the woods that has the scent of damp moss and roots, and singing to herself as the backyard is sunny and calm. She has three dolls that are about the same size as her hands, a Mommy, Daddy, and Baby doll. She puts the Mommy and Daddy doll in one car and has them hug each other. "Love and kiss, love and kiss," she sings. Then she puts the Baby doll in another car and she has the Baby doll's car crash into Mommy's and Daddy's car, turning it over, killing both the Mommy and Daddy. The Baby doll treks over to the car and picks up the Daddy doll and he wakes up and they stick their arms around each other. "Love and kiss, love and kiss," she sings again, and the Baby and the Daddy drive away in the Baby's car to the house made of four sticks she has placed in a square, with an opening for the doorway. She puts Daddy and Baby in the house, and

Daddy sits on the ground and grows breasts and Baby sucks milk from his breasts. Then she picks up the Mommy where she lies by the side of the road, and she wakes her up and Mommy starts to cry, and Baby says, "Here, eat this caca and shut up before I really give you something to cry about," and she feeds the Mommy some poisoned caca and the Mommy falls onto the grass and dies again. The baby goes back to the Daddy and kisses him, and the Daddy and Baby hug each other and are very happy, and then Ariel drops them and sits back against the trunk of the tree sucking her thumb.

At the usual time when the sun has settled on the hills like a huge red rubber ball, Daddy comes walking around the side of the house, neatly attired in his white suit, his White Panama hat, his red tie, and his brown leather sandals. She jumps to her feet and skips toward him, screaming "Daddy, Daddy, Daddy!" and he swoops her off the ground and spins her around, his strong hands under her arms, so that she swoons with fear and joy. "How's my little princesa?" he asks in the majestic Spanish that dances from his tongue and embraces the air, a language that is strong and warm, not like the cold English that bolts from Mother's lips.

He sits down on the lawn chair and she climbs onto his lap, throwing one leg over his large thigh and pulling herself up, her yellow cotton dress falling back to reveal her white panties. She looks up into his twinkling eyes and squeals, "Mi padre!", speaking to him in Spanish. "My Daddy Daddy Daddy!" He smiles at her with his big, suave Daddy face, his eyes confident and strong and knowing like the eyes of a young god, sitting so straight with his chest held high and his neck arched, and his voice deep and powerful.

"Oops!" he says, pulling down her skirt. "Look what I see."

"No," she replies. "It's not!"

"Yes, it is!"

"Daddy. My Daddy," she says. "Let me see your penis."

"I've told you, that's impossible."

"But I want to see it."

"When you grow up you can see your husband's penis."

"I want to see it."

"No, no, no."

She reaches toward his crotch, smiling gleefully. "I can touch it, Daddy. Yes, I can."

"No, no, no."

"Yes, yes, yes." She feels that if she can see or touch her Daddy's penis, something special, something magical will happen. There will be a miraculous change inside her. Perhaps she will grow her own penis, or have baby penises inside her belly and under other places in her skin, and they will feel warm and strong and she will feel safe from the monster mother. Without a penis of her own, her monster mother can devour her. Daddy can give her a penis if he wants to. "I'm going to touch it," she squeals. "I'm going to touch my Daddy's penis."

He picks her up in his arms like a twig and rocks her wildly and tosses her up into the air and catches her as she squeals. "Shall I throw you into the trees? Into the tops of the trees with the crows and hawks?"

"Yes! Throw me, my Daddy."

He stands and swings her outward in an arc and she screams. Then he sits down and she rests in his lap.

"Daddy, Daddy. Are you my Daddy?"

"Of course I'm your Daddy." He beams at her with his white teeth.

"Are you all my Daddy?" She means to ask if he is only her Daddy and no one's else's. He understands.

"*Of course. I'm not the Daddy of a lizard. I'm not the Daddy of a monkey. I'm only your Daddy.*"

"*I love my Daddy.*" *She buries her nose in his shirt and breathes in his strong, Daddy smell of wool and sweat and leather, and he kisses her with little pecks all over her face. He is her big, tall, happy Daddy who knows every-thing, and she giggles into his eyes.* "*My Daddy. I love my Daddy, yes I do.*"

"*And Daddy loves his* princesa.*"

"*Daddy, may I sleep in your bed tonight?*"

"*Why do you want to sleep in my bed?*"

"*Please.*"

"*But why?*"

"*Please, let me, Daddy. Please.*"

"*Are you afraid?*"

"*Yes. I'm afraid of the monster.*"

"*What monster?*"

"*Please, Daddy. Please.*"

"*Your Mommy's not a monster. You shouldn't talk that way.*"

"*Please let me sleep with you, Daddy. Please.*"

"*But you're going to be a big girl now.*"

And then the sound of Mommy's Porsche, the tires flinging gravel down the driveway, and Ariel looks at her Daddy and he looks at her, and he is smiling, his brows raised, his teeth sparkling, and he is thinking about the mother and no longer thinking about Ariel even though he is looking at her. "*Well, there's Mommy now.*" *Mother trots around the house, her dark, wavy hair—the same thick hair as her daughter's—flapping in the breeze, the leather schoolbook satchel dangling under one arm. A yellow monarch butterfly lands on her head for a mo-ment, crowning her, blessing her, and then flies off in a flurry as the mother drifts toward them in slow motion. Daddy dumps Ariel on the ground and rushes into his wife's arms, and she presses her body against his, drop-ping the satchel, as Ariel looks on, leaning way back to see their radiant faces as they kiss. She feels jealous, left out, and catches onto her father's left leg. Mommy and Daddy finish kissing and turn to Ariel, arm in arm, smiling down at her, and her Daddy says, "You see, Ariel, Mommy's a good Mommy, aren't you, Mommy?"*

"Of course she is," Mommy says, squatting down to pat Ariel's head. "And Mommy loves her Ariel."

Ariel turns and runs off toward the house.

"Ariel?" her Mommy calls. "What's the matter with her? Sometimes I just don't understand her."

"She's just full of energy," her Daddy says. "She's just full of youthful energy."

Ariel, now 7, lies arm-in-arm with her younger sister Florence, who has just turned 4. They can hear their mother's voice in the other room, shrieking at their father. They can hear their father pleading softly with their mother. Ariel is afraid.

"Don't worry," Florence says. "She won't hurt you."

"You can't stop her," Ariel says. "Nobody can."

"I can scream," Florence proclaims.

"She can scream louder."

"I'm not scared of her."

"You're so brave. You're much braver than I am."

Outside the window an almost full, orange-colored Chilean moon floats just above the hills beyond the woods. It shines across the faces of the two girls so that their four brown eyes glow in the dark.

"I'm not so brave," Florence says.

"You're very brave."

"Mommy wants to hurt you."

"She doesn't hurt me anymore. I don't pay attention to her."

"Mommy's not nice."

"She can't help it."

"Mommy's a monster."

"She's not a monster. She just can't control herself."

Ariel has been a mother to Florence. She has helped Maria change Florence's diapers and later has helped teach Florence to use the potty. She has held her when she cried and talked to her when she wanted to talk. She has soothed her the way she herself would like to have been soothed, and sometimes it feels as if they are one person against the world. Florence loves Ariel for taking care of her and Ariel loves Florence for supporting her battle with her mother, and the two them are always together.

They lie silently for a while, listening to their mother's voice down the hallway in her bedroom. In times past, to calm their fears, they have cried out themselves at the shrillness of their mother's voice. Tonight they merely wait in frozen silence for what they know is going to happen.

Now the voice comes nearer, ricocheting down the hallway.

Now the door juts open.

Now the two sisters look at one another.

"Well, well, well," the mother says, bounding into the room in one motion. "What have we here?"

"Leave her alone," Florence says.

"The little monster and her assistant planning schemes no doubt."

"Leave her alone!"

The mother hovers huge and ugly above them, smiling at Florence and then at Ariel. "So, you've managed to turn Flo against me, is that it? While I'm away at the university you're turning your younger sister into your assistant monster. Don't look at me like that, with your innocent, accusatory eyes. Don't look at me as if I'm the monster. Anyway, if I'm one, you're one too. We're just alike, you and me. Aren't we dear? Aren't we? Answer me when I'm speaking to you!" The mother leans close to Ariel, grinning. "Can you talk?" Ariel does not do anything to stop her, nor does she show any sign of pain. She does not fly out of her body as she has in the past; she stays inside herself, yet she is not herself. She looks at her mother with a resigned, world-weary expression, and thinks about nothing.

"Stop it!" Florence exclaims, leaping up on slightly bowed legs. She heaves into her mother, pushing at her thighs with both hands. "Stop it! Stop it, Mama, right now!"

The mother pays no attention to Florence, merely flicking her away with one arm. Her entire focus is still on Ariel. "What? Nothing to say? Of course not. Miss Princess doesn't deign to talk. Miss Princess is above all the rest of us."

"Mama! Stop it!" Florence stands with her hands on her hips. "I mean it. Leave Ariel alone. Leave her alone right now."

"Oh, poor Ariel. Poor, poor Ariel. Mama's picking on Daddy's little princess."

"I said stop it!"

"Why should I stop when nobody ever stops for me?"

"STOP IT!" Florence screams, pushing at her mother's thighs.

The mother smiles bitterly and waves the two daughters away and careens out of the room, slamming the door so hard that the whole room flinches. Ariel pulls her blankets tightly around herself and turns away and thinks, I don't care about this, I don't care about anything. I don't care about her or the trees or the sky or anything. I don't care that Daddy is always gone.

"It's all right now," Florence says, throwing a protec-

*tive arm around her. "She won't come back again to-
night."*

"Probably not."

"You're not a monster."

"Thanks."

"I won't let her hurt you."

"I know you won't."

*The two lie together gazing out of the window at the
moonlight. Ariel can feel her sister snuggle up behind her
and she tries to sigh the sadness away. I don't want to cry,
she thinks. I have to be strong and hard so nobody can
hurt me. If I cry I'll be weak. I'll never cry. Never. She
closes her eyes and tries to go to sleep, but she is awake
long after Florence has dozed off and her breath is hot
against her cheek. I don't care about anything, she
repeats. I don't care. I don't care. I don't care.*

Ariel talked about her childhood for a week. For five
straight sessions she talked of it, and seemed suddenly
absorbed with it. As she talked about it, she became more
and more depressed. Gone was the sulky, seductive demeanor of the first few weeks. Now she seemed the
perfect psychoanalytic patient, serious and introspective
and insightful. "It's amazing," she said again and again. "I
can't believe that it really happened to me." And, at other
times, "I never knew I had all these memories inside me."

"Should I confront my parents about these memories?"
she asked one day.

"What for?"

"I just feel so angry at them."

"Do you really think they'll be receptive?"

"No, not really."

However, she confronted them anyway, perhaps partly
out of guilt, to let them know she had been talking about

them. When she did, they suggested that I was trying to turn her against them. This made her doubt her own memories.

"Why is it," she asked, "that my parents seem to be so well-adjusted? If they're as monstrous as I remember them, how can they be so contented with each other and happy? I mean, they're both respected professionals, with hordes of friends, and seem so in love. Maybe I'm just making up all these memories? Maybe I'm an ungrateful, spoiled brat who's vilifying her parents?"

"Maybe you are."

"Do you really mean that?"

"Do you?"

"I may be spoiled and sometimes I'm a brat. But I didn't make it up. It happened."

"Are you sure?"

"How could they be both sick and well adjusted? Shouldn't sick people be miserable?"

She was distractedly fiddling with her ring as she talked. Her inability to make sense of the paradox of her parents' behavior represented the intellectual aspect of her defense of splitting. She had begun splitting them into good and bad parents in order to protect the sanctity of the good parent image so as not to feel completely terrorized. As long as she could tell herself that the monster Mommy and the betrayer Daddy were not her real Mommy and Daddy, she could maintain some semblance of safety. Now, in therapy, she was confronted with this split in how she saw them, and with her inability to integrate them and make sense of their behavior.

"I was just thinking that you used the word *seem* in describing your parents as being well adjusted and happy," I said.

"Did I say that? I suppose that's true. Yes, they seem well adjusted, but perhaps they aren't really so well adjusted. A lot of people seem well adjusted on the surface. The Nazis in Germany seemed well adjusted to one another. I once read that they were quite happy and even vibrant during the years when they were torturing and killing Jews, quite loving and generous with one another, throwing parties and giving lavish gifts and living the carefree life."

"Was that how it was with your parents?"

"Oh, yes. They were always socializing, always full of *joie de vivre,* and never understanding why I was so unhappy. . . ." She went silent. "I just had a terrible thought."

"What's that?"

"My parents were Nazis. They were maintaining their well-being at my expense. I was their Jew." She held her hands over her ears and closed her eyes. "I think I always knew that, but only now could I say it." She began to cry for the first time.

The following Monday she drifted exhaustedly through my doorway and sat on the chair. Her face was drawn, her skin pale, her demeanor wan. She sat hunched over and did not look at me. She kept her coat wrapped around her and sat very still, so that the jacket made her puffed up like a frightened bird.

"I had another one of my rages this Saturday night," she said, glancing up at me.

"What happened?"

"I sat on the floor in the bathroom holding a knife against my wrist for a few hours. My roommate Beatrice and my friend Jim finally talked me out of it."

"What about our agreement?"

"What agreement?"

"We made an agreement when you first started therapy that if you ever felt suicidal you'd call me."

"Oh, that. I didn't think about it. Anyway, I was too

distracted. I was angry at my father because he always says such stupid things to me on the phone. Every time I try to talk to him about things he quotes from Sartre or Camus. He thinks he's such a decent, sensible man, and he's really such a hypocrite and liar. All men are liars, really. They all pretend to care about women, they all pretend to be such feminists, but they're really not.''

"But what about our agreement? *You* lied to me. You said you'd call me if you were suicidal and you didn't. What about that?"

"I forgot." She pursed her lips, as though I were making too much of it. "Anyway, it was midnight Saturday night. I didn't want to disturb you."

"But we had an agreement. What are you resisting, Ariel?"

"I guess I didn't want to make myself vulnerable to a man."

"You'd rather die than make yourself vulnerable to a man?"

"Maybe so."

That was part of it, I thought, but not all of it. The other part of it was that her rages really did not constitute serious suicidal threats, but were primarily done for dramatic effect; therefore, she did not see a need to call me.

After a while she lay down on the couch and related a recurring dream. She was on a subway platform that looked like the subway in London. There were men in uniform all around, and when she looked closely at their uniforms she saw that they all had Nazi insignia. She suddenly felt afraid for her life and began to run toward the stairs. On the way she saw a man who looked like Hitler. She ran past him and bounded up the stairs and then awoke, terrified.

She had had this dream the night after she had compared her parents to Nazis. The dream was about her parents and about her feeling that she had been imprisoned and abused by them like a Jew in a concentration camp. The Hitler in the dream represented her father—her split-off, bad, hypocritical, evil Daddy who in her primitive unconscious fantasies was just as monstrous as her bad Mommy. The fact that the dream took place in London was an allusion to the time when her father had to flee Chile and the family was exiled to London, during her early adolescence. She had often described this period as "being in Siberia." The fact that it took place in the London subway, known to Londoners as "The Tube," is perhaps meant to symbolize a womb; she is trapped in her mother's "tubes," and her father (Hitler) won't help her out. Instead he keeps her imprisoned.

After giving her this interpretation, she said, "That's very interesting. I never thought of that."

A few days later she came in feeling enraged at men. "Men are so stupid," she said. "They don't know anything about politics. It's amazing how little they know, but they think they know it all." She half looked around to weigh my reaction. "Beatrice and I were at a bar last night with Pete and Jim and Ralph and they were acting so stupid. It's really amazing how stupid men can be at times. Particularly American men. Particularly American, white, Anglo-Saxon Protestant men." She spat out these last sentences with a smile of glee, then paused to ask, "Do you think I'm exaggerating?"

I knew that whenever she complained about American men it was indirectly a barb aimed at me. Adding the new phrase about WASPs (she assumed I was one) served to up the ante. "Is there some reason why I would think you're exaggerating?"

"No, I was just asking. But it's true. American men don't know anything about politics. Last night Jim and Pete and Ralph were trying to act as if they were liberals and progressive, but then they were trying to argue that it didn't matter how many women were in politics. Can you imagine that? How can you call yourself a progressive and a liberal and then argue that it doesn't matter how many women are in politics? Am I making sense? They kept saying that it had nothing to do with sexism, and when Beatrice and I poked holes in their arguments, you could just see their little male egos jumping up and down. You could see their egos jumping up and down like rabbits. Do you think I'm exaggerating?" she asked.

"I wonder why you keep asking that?" I said.

"I don't know. Maybe I'm wondering if you're a feminist."

"And if I say I am?"

"I wouldn't believe you. Men say that all the time, because they know it's what women want to hear."

"And if I say I'm not a feminist?"

"I'd believe you."

"So no matter what I say, you're convinced I'm a sexist? I can't win."

"Actually, though, I don't think you're a sexist. You're a therapist."

It was clear that in some respects she both idealized and neutered me; if I were a man I would be a sexist, but because I was a therapist, I was not a man but some idealized, gender-neutral, maternal father-symbol. What this told me was that the best way to relate to her as a therapist was simply to provide her with a safe space and join her the way she wanted to be joined. She wanted me to join her fantasy—play the rescuing maternal father to the cinderella daughter, be the selfobject she needed in order to bring about the necessary transmuting idealizations (Kohut 1971). This was what she had needed but not gotten from her father. I knew she was always acting, and that there was no cohesive self. Therefore, in order to begin to establish this cohesive self, I had to meet her at the level of fantasy; I had to accept her the way she wanted to be accepted for now. At the same time I recognized how volatile she could be, and knew that at any moment the borderline transference might shift from idealization to devaluation. She might then view me the same way she viewed other men—in derogatory terms.

Indeed, her idealization of me was always fragile and she could never trust it completely, just as she could never trust her idealized father (he always let her down). She had to continually test it out by attempting to seduce me, as she did with all men. If she could seduce me, that would prove that I was not a neutral, maternal father-symbol whom she could trust, but just another man. In that case she would be able to rage against and devalue me as a sexist male. I knew this would happen sooner or later, even if I did not succumb to seduction; indeed, not succumbing would be a narcissistic injury as well and would likewise engender her rage. Therefore, I was prepared to switch from joining to confrontation if and when the rage was directed at me.

There was also another factor that had to be taken into account. A therapy relationship does not happen in a vacuum. Both Ariel and I were the products of our times and could not help but be affected by the social currents of our times. Feminism was a powerful social force, the manifestations of which could be seen daily on television, in books, in the movies, in government, and in education. In terms of her own development, feminism—particularly the militant brand that views men as responsible for all the problems of women—tended to encourage Ariel's own anger at and devaluation of men. It represented a "higher authority" that gave her permission for her derogative opinions of men. At the same time, it was a threat to the therapy and to me, supporting her tendency of splitting and viewing people in terms of symbols. Hence, supported by militant feminism, she could see me as a white Protestant male and make associated projective identifications, knowing that the "culture" was behind her. On my part it aroused occasional impulses of what I have elsewhere (Schoenewolf 1993) termed "cultural counterresistance." I resented being viewed by militant feminists as a symbolic white Protestant male rather than as a human being, resented the almost daily accusations about male oppression, sexism, rape, sexual harassment, and patriarchy that filled the air waves, resented students coming to my college courses and trying to get me fired because I did not have enough women writers in my syllabus, and resented having editors reject my writing because I had used politically incorrect language (such as "maternal deprivation" rather than "caretaker deprivation"). This resentment caused me to have less tolerance toward Ariel's propensity for devaluating men along militant feminist lines, so that now and then I would find myself having an impulse to counter some of her provocative remarks, or an inability to listen with as much empathy as I might otherwise.

Added to this mix was the prevailing notion—also coming from feminism—that women should not go into therapy with male therapists. She brought this up at one point, saying that her friends did not understand why she was in therapy with a male. At the time she brought it up she was still idealizing me so that it was not an immediate issue and I was not called upon to defend or justify her being in therapy with me. However, I understood that, once brought up, it was still lurking in the background, ready to become an issue if and when necessary. I also understood that the "sisterhood" of militant feminism represented a generalized mother transference; just as her own mother resented and tried to interfere with her relationship with her father and keep her bound to herself, so the feminist "sisterhood" attempts to keep women from bonding with men in general and with male therapists in particular.

As therapists, we often forget about the societal context, but in fact it should be taken into consideration. So when Ariel continued to talk about her anger at men and about their sexism, I would first bring it back to her relationship with me, and then trace it back to her relationship with her father. It was a delicate matter to try to get her to let go of her primitive symbolization and see me for the human being that I actually was, how I was actually relating to her, and how I was actually caring about her, as distinguished from the militant feminist view of me as threatening male figure. Then it was just as delicate to get her to see her generalized father transference and trace it back to its source.

"How about your father? Was he a sexist?" I asked her one day.

"My father? He's the ultimate sexist."

"What do you mean?"

"He thinks he's superior to all women. He makes me so angry."

We discussed his sexism, my sexism, sexism in general, and then she finally got beyond that to some memories. Her eyes narrowed and her voice became thoughtful as she recalled the days of her adolescence.

Ariel in the library. She is 14 years old. Her father sits behind his desk. He is 39 years old. He is smiling calmly.

"But Papa, you don't understand," she is telling him. She is restless in her chair, a skinny, nervous child-woman with dark, solemnly searching eyes. "I feel like killing myself. I feel like I don't want to live anymore. I feel like everything's hopeless."

"I know, I know," he says, nodding very quickly. *"Misery is part of life. It is an inescapable part of life."*

"But I'm miserable for a reason. I'm miserable because of you and because of Mama. You never take me seriously, and she won't let me be. I feel . . . smothered."

"I understand. Your mother has her moods. But she doesn't mean anything by it. We both love you very much. If we smother you, it is because we love you."

"Whether she means something or not, she makes me miserable. When are you going to talk to her? You keep saying you'll talk to her."

"I will talk to her. I promise you I will. However, neither your mother nor I is the real cause of your misery. We only appear to be the cause." He pulls a book out of the library. It is a deluxe volume with gold-leafed pages by Sartre. *"You see this book? You should read it. You should read the existential writers. What you're going through is a phase, an adolescent phase. Your desire to kill yourself springs from an existential dread. This existential dread can be made worse by what happens in our environment, but it will always be there, in good times and bad. It's part of the human condition."*

"I don't think that's what I'm feeling."

"Have you not told me that sometimes at night you wake up from a nightmare and feel terrified? But you do not know of what you are terrified?"

"Yes, but . . ."

"That's it. That's the existential dread."

"But I feel terrified after a nightmare about monsters or killers chasing me. It has nothing to do with existentialism."

"The monsters and killers represent death. It is the fear of death, the recognition of our own mortality, that lies beneath existential dread."

"So you think my misery is just a fear of death? I don't get it."

"You see, the fear of death is also connected to the recognition that there is no God in heaven to look over us. We are all responsible for our own fate. It is this knowledge that we are mortal, that there is no God, which produces the existential dread and which makes us feel abandoned. It causes the violent mood swings, the desire to take our own lives. This violent mood swing is particularly bad in adolescence. Believe me, I know all about it. When I was your age my moods would change from day to day. One day I'd feel as though I were the king of the universe, and the next I wanted to shoot myself. But I outgrew it and you will too." Her father leans back in his chair and folds his arms. "Do you understand?"

"Yes, I think so."

"You think so?"

"Yes, I understand."

"What do you understand?"

"I understand . . . that what I'm feeling is existential dread or something like that."

Her father shakes his head and rolls back his eyes. The two of them sit looking at one another. Around them, on every wall, are her father's books, carefully arranged according to subject matter. The books seem to be the boundary and definition of his relationship with her. On the far wall is a grandfather clock, ticking loudly, as though to underscore the passing of time as they sit silently in a room of writings by the grandfathers of the world. "Read the book, then we'll talk."

"All right. I'll read it." Ariel slumps down in her chair. Her father is a brilliant man. He is the Secretary of the Treasury. He holds two Ph.D.'s. He has read thousands of books. His words are logical. His tone is confident and *stubborn. How can she dispute him? "I guess you're right," she says. "It's probably existential dread. I hope so. But, all the same, you will talk to Mama, won't you?"*

"Of course, of course."

She leaves the library feeling vaguely reassured. By the time she has slipped into her room and fallen onto her bed and thought about what her father has said, the doubts creep in. Before long the vague reassurance gives way to a confusion, then to a feeling of nausea. Ah, the nausea, she thinks. That must be from the dread. Didn't Sartre write a book called Nausea? *Papa must be right. Yes, it's the dread.*

She remembers her father's calm smile, and his refusal to take seriously anything that she was trying to tell him about her mother or about himself. The nausea becomes worse. No, she thinks, it's not existential dread. He does *it. He* makes *me sick. He never listens to a thing I'm trying to tell him. Neither does she.*

No, no, no, it's me, she thinks. I'm no good. I'm a monster. I'm full of hateful feelings and I'm trying to blame them on my parents. How can they be at fault? They are pillars of the community. It must be me. I should just kill myself and get it over with. I'm no good to anybody.

She sinks into her bed, her arms wrapped around herself as her thoughts skip from side to side. Now it is existential dread that makes her sick; now it is her father. Now she feels angry at her parents. Now she feels guilty for being angry at her parents. Now she feels angry for feeling guilty for being angry at her parents. Around and around her mind goes, and it never ever stops.

Now she is 15 and she can like herself in the mirror. Boys notice her. Girls adore her. The telephone rings all day

*long. She embraces all who come to her, collects friends
the way others might collect stamps or old coins. Maybe if
I have enough friends, she thinks, I will be safe. Maybe if
enough people love me, my parents will see that I'm not a
monster after all.*

*It is summer and each morning the phone rings and a
new friend is inviting her out.*

*"Are you going out again?" her mother asks, rushing
down the stairs as Ariel talks on the phone. "Who's that?
Tanya? Do you think you should get so close to her? She
seems a bit odd to me. Don't you notice something odd
about her?"*

"No, Mama. She's perfectly fine."

*"You should stay at home today. You're always fran-
tically going about. Why don't you stay home and paint?
If you want to go to art school someday, you'll need to
develop a portfolio."*

"I will, I will."

*"Don't you think Tanya is a bit odd, dear?" she asks
Ariel's father.*

"Yes, now that I think about it," he says.

*After a while Ariel drops Tanya and becomes friends
with Angela. Now she is often on the phone with Angela.*

*"Angela again? There's something about that girl," her
mother says, rushing down the stairs. "Something missing. I can't put my finger on it."*

*It happens again and again; as soon as she gets close to
somebody, her mother finds fault with her, and then Ariel
begins to look for reasons to pull out of the friendship. It
is even worse with boys.*

*One boy in particular, Juan, begins to call. He calls
every morning and every evening. They walk to school
together. They walk home together. He sits with her on
their front lawn. She tells him about her loneliness, her
fear, her anger, and about how she wants to kill herself.*

He tells her of his anger at his parents. They walk into the woods behind her house. A flock of geese flies over their heads squawking and she is startled, grabbing his arm. They lie on the cool dank green moss. They kiss. They fondle. He lies on top of her. She has never felt so fine, so safe, so free. For a few moments she can forget everything. He wedges himself between her legs and says he adores her. She is gazing up at the trees and the leaves rattling in the wind and she hears the geese flapping their wings above the trees and he is inside her and he fills her emptiness, melts her loneliness, soothes her rage, and she feels as though she is flying the way she imagined she could fly as a child, high on the top of the woods. She cries out with surprised desperation, "I love you, Juan, I revere you, I worship you . . ." and the sound of her voice seems to mesmerize the woods for a split second, so that all its inhabitants, squirrels and macaws, lizards and armadillos, monkeys and frogs, freeze and fall silent in the green-wooded sunlight. And she says it a hundred times, whisperingly, clinging to him as though she would hold on to him forever, until he finally pulls away and smiles at her with question-mark eyes, "Are you all right? Ariel? What?"

"Yes, yes, yes. I could see the tops of the trees. I could smell the chlorophyll."

"Ariel?"

"It was all minty and warm from the sun."

He sends roses and mums. He writes corny verse about her dark eyes like smoldering embers. He brings stuffed animals with gold rings attached to the ears. He calls her several times a day.

Her mother rushes down the stairs.

"Ariel, who's that on the phone? Is that Juan again? Don't you think he's a bit old for you? And he always has

such a strange look in his eyes, as though he had just seen a ghost."

"No, Mama, I don't think he's strange. That's just him."

"But you're too young to get so involved with a boy. You're only 15. You don't want to get so involved and mess things up. You should be seeing other boys, playing the field."

"Your mother's right," her father says, standing at her side. "You shouldn't be so involved. Why don't you come with us to the beach house this weekend?"

"I don't want to go to the beach house," Ariel says.

"Why don't you both leave her alone," Florence says from the top of the stairs.

"Stay out of it," her father says.

"She'd rather have sex with her boyfriend, Papa," her brother Raul says, poking his head above the railing.

"Watch your tongue," the father says.

"The beach house, the beach house," her younger brother Luis says.

"It'll be a family outing," the mother says.

"Bueno, bueno," the father says. *"Then it's settled. Call Juan and tell him we're going to the beach house."*

"I'm not going," Ariel says, running to her room.

"It's not healthy to spend so much time with Juan," her mother calls about her.

"Your mother's right. Your mother's always right," the father says.

"I can't stand it!" she screams. She is 16 and poised in the kitchen with a knife in her hands. "I can't stand it anymore. Nobody ever listens to me."

"Ariel, put down the knife," Raul says. He is five years

*younger than her, but he acts as though he is her superior.
He has the same stern brown eyes as his father. "Papa,
you'd better come in here. Ariel's having one of her fits
again."*

Her father rushes forth, sternly.

*"Ariel, give me the knife." He looks at her with his
brown eyes. "Give it to me right now."*

*"That's all you care about, the knife. You don't care
about me. Only about the knife. Are you afraid I'll
scratch the furniture with it? Is that it?" She smiles and
holds the knife toward the oak cabinets. "Are you afraid
I'll kill myself and cause a scandal that will make the
family look bad?"*

"Ariel, give it to me."

*"How will things look, right? That's all you're con-
cerned about. No. I'm going to kill myself. I'm going to
make such a hideous mess that all of Santiago will be
appalled. The Secretary of the Treasury's daughter splat-
ters her blood all over the Secretary's new white suit."*

"Stop talking that way."

*"I can't stand being alive anymore. You just don't
understand. I really can't stand it!" She can feel the rage
throbbing inside her. It is always throbbing inside her.
She does not understand the rage. She does not understand why she always has to feel it. The slightest look from
either parent, the slightest twist in their voices, can set her
off. Her brothers, who always side with them, can also set
her off. She feels surrounded by them all, overwhelmed,
suffocated, powerless. There seems to be nothing she can
do to protect herself from them. Whenever she tries to
complain, they tell her she is making too much of things
or going through a phase or experiencing existential
dread. If she has a fit, they tell her she's crazy. The rage
goes on and on and there seems to be no way out. It
constantly fills her body and eats away at her*

innards like acid. She gets stomach pains and headaches. She knows something is very wrong, but nobody will listen. Even when she has a fit, they do not take her seriously. The only way out is to kill them or myself, she thinks, and aims the knife toward her wrist. "I'm going to end it right now!" she smiles.

"Stop it," her father says, and takes the arm with the knife, twisting it until the knife falls to the floor.

"Stupido!" she screams, and pumps away at him with her fists. Then one by one she opens the doors of the kitchen cabinets and empties their contents, tossing pots and pans, glasses and bowls, cans of beans and peas and sprouts, boxes of cereal and corn meal, jars of salt and spice, onto the floor, where they spin and clatter and spill in all directions.

"What's the matter with you!" her father moans dumb-foundedly.

"She's crazy," her brother says.

"It's the dread, Papa, the dread has got me," she replies, smiling. She sings to the tune of a popular song: "That existential dread has got me in its spell, that existential dread that you weave so well . . ."

"Crazy," the younger brother repeats.

She stops talking to her mother, father, and brothers. She talks only to Florence and to her friends. Her days are spent counting minutes and seconds of silence.

"Ariel, don't you think it's silly to go on with this silent treatment?" her mother asks at breakfast.

"Those who speak do not know," she replies, quoting a Chinese philosopher. "And those who know do not speak."

"What is that supposed to mean?"

"Eat your eggs before they get cold," Maria says.

She does not reply. Her fried eggs stare at her like big yellow monster eyes. She stabs the eyes with her fork, smiling.

"I said, what is that supposed to mean?" her mother asks.

She rises without looking at her mother or Maria or Florence or her brothers and runs wordlessly out of the house to catch the bus for school.

She tells all her friends that her parents are impossible and that she cannot stand to talk with them. Her friends are her friends, but they do not really understand. To them her parents seem wonderful. Whenever they come to her house her parents joke with them and seem so very jovial and good-humored. Her friends do not see her mother at night. They do not know how her father says this and says that and says nothing. They do not know the daily life of the household. She feels isolated even among her friends. The only person she can really be honest with is Florence. But she has taught Florence everything she knows, so she can never be sure if Florence's support of her is real or simply a trained response. After all, if everybody else—her parents, her brothers, her friends— thinks she is not seeing things correctly, how can she trust it when her younger sister says she is? There is nobody to trust, no place to turn, nothing to do but remain silent.

"Ariel's not talking," her mother says to her father in the evening.

"It's just a phase," her father says.

She walks by them and they drink their martinis.

At 17 she begins to talk again, but she stops eating. If she must give the world her words, then she will no longer let it enter her body. She must draw a boundary somewhere, so it seems to her on her deepest and most reactive level of

being, or the world will totally intrude on her and
overwhelm her. However, she does not think this in
words. In words she thinks only of being thin and of the
benefits of being thin and the hazards of being fat. All
day long she thinks about how classy it is to be thin. She
wants to be beautiful and thin like her mother, not fat
and vulgar like Maria. She wants to be admired, not
disdained. Her fantasies are about being beautiful and
thin in New York. Her dreams are about being beautiful
and thin in paradise. All her friends are concerned about
being thin. All of Chile is concerned about being thin.
Thinness is everything. Thinness is everywhere.

She writes a poem:

> Oh, let me be as thin as a falling leaf
> That drifts across the wind;
> Let me fall blindly and freely through the air
> So that the wind can rock me
> Wise and wordless in the afternoon sun
> So that I might at long last
> Be kissed by the carefree earth
> And die in its cool arms.

Her father and mother take her to many physicians
who say nothing is wrong with her. Then they take her to
a friend who is a psychiatrist. Her mother tells the
therapist that Ariel has a problem with self-control. Her
father says it is an adolescent existential search for
meaning. Ariel sits slumped over, sandwiched between
father and mother, her eyes to the floor.

After her mother and father have left her alone with the
therapist, Ariel says, "Sometimes I think maybe I'm just
angry at my parents."

"No," the therapist replies, smiling confidently. "It's
not your parents. I've known them a long time. Your

*mother and I belong to the same women's club. Your
father and I went to the same school. It's most likely your
peer group. You feel what we call peer pressure. You and
your friends are competing to see who can be the thin-
nest."*

"But I feel so much anger toward my parents."

"That's normal. Most teenagers do."

*"Sometimes I want to kill them. Sometimes I want to
kill myself."*

"I understand."

"So you think it's just peer pressure?"

"Absolutely."

*Dr. Rodriguez is logical and confident like her father,
and Ariel cannot argue with her, so she talks about the
peer pressure and she talks about gaining weight and
developing a positive attitude and making good grades
and other things Dr. Rodriguez wants her to talk about.
For a while it is pleasant to go twice a week to her office
and talk for an hour. At least somebody is listening to
her. In fact, Dr. Rodriguez takes a great deal of interest in
her, just as everybody seems to do, and becomes very keen
on helping her to become a well-adjusted teenager. In her
zeal Dr. Rodriguez begins to listen less and less and to
offer more and more advice. Ariel begins coming late for
sessions and then missing them completely.*

*After a year she is bored with the therapy and stops
going altogether. She is not so sure she wants to be that
adjusted, and anyway she has decided that Dr. Rodriguez
is too old and fat to really understand her teenage
problems or her eating problems. When she announces to
her parents that she has quit therapy her parents are, of
course, supportive. Sitting on the living room couch, they
clink their brandy glasses.*

*"I always thought it was just a phase. You don't need
a therapist," her father says.*

"Let me give you a big hug," her mother says, gushing toward Ariel and enveloping her in her arms.

For some time I had been getting secondhand reports about Ariel's relationship with Beatrice. Then one day she brought Beatrice to the office and I was able to get a firsthand view.

They came into my office and sat side by side in my two chairs, dressed alike in baggy, wrinkly jeans and plaid shirts that hung over their jeans. Neither wore makeup or jewelry and both had mussy hair, although Beatrice's hair was blond rather than brown, and a bit shorter than Ariel's.

There was a long, awkward silence, and the two of them grinned and giggled and gawked at me. I pulled up my chair and sat facing them, looking from one to another, waiting for one of them to speak, meanwhile sizing up Beatrice. She was not as feminine or pretty as Ariel. There was a masculine quality in her rigid movements and her square jaw and in a certain hardness around the eyes. Her eyes were a cold blue, and they looked at you fleetingly, without feeling, like lion's eyes. I felt afraid of her.

Ariel and Beatrice grinned at each other uncomfortably. "Do you want to talk or should I?" she asked her friend.

"You talk," Beatrice said rather softly. Her manner was secretive. For the most part she kept her eyes down and seemed not to want me to hear her voice or include me.

"The reason Beatrice came in today is because we thought, well actually I thought, that maybe you could help her. As you know, when we got back from our trip in the fall, Beatrice had a breakdown, she became suicidal, and we had to take her to Bellevue." Ariel and Beatrice glanced at one another in a secretive way. I was wondering what had happened on that trip, but I did not have time to ask. "At Bellevue Beatrice was assigned this psychiatrist who would just look at her disdainfully and warn her to take her medication. She kept seeing him for a while after she left Bellevue even though she didn't like him and didn't think he really cared about her. I mean, he didn't really seem to understand her or want to understand her." Another secretive glance. "Then she went home to Ohio to live with her parents, and while she was there she saw another therapist, but this therapist just kept saying stupid, parental things like 'You have to learn to control yourself,' and giving her idiotic sermons. And so she called me and asked what to do and I said come back to New York, maybe my therapist will be able to refer you to somebody like him. And so she came back." They smiled at one another. "Anyway, she had to return to New York so we could finish our novel. It's almost finished, it just needs a little rewriting and editing. Everybody who's read it is fascinated by it, so we're hoping we can get it published soon. Anyway, Beatrice is back and we thought maybe you might know somebody who works like you do, or maybe even you could work with her yourself, if that's ethical."

"It's not a question of ethics. Whether or not I work with Beatrice or refer her to somebody else depends mostly on whether or not it would be therapeutically viable for both of you to work with me. What kinds of feelings would you have working with the same therapist?" They grinned at one another for a long time as if conversing with their thoughts. "How would you both feel about that?"

"I'd feel all right," Ariel said. "I think it could be good, actually."

Beatrice did not answer. "What about you, Beatrice?"

"I don't know. I'd have to think about it," Beatrice said, so softly that I could scarcely hear her.

"I'm sorry. What was the last thing you said?"

"I'd have to think about it," she repeated, and looked at me as though I were stupid not to have heard her.

"What do you need to think about?"

"I'm not sure how I feel about you. I'm not sure how I'd feel about working with the same therapist as Ariel."

"You're not sure . . . I'm sorry, could you please speak up?"

Beatrice looked at Ariel in disgust. Ariel spoke for her. "She said she's not sure how she'd feel about seeing my therapist. She wants to think about it."

"That's understandable. Anyway, I know some other therapists who work in a similar way and I'd be glad to give you a referral. The point is that you need to find the right therapist for you, one with whom you click. That's very important. You need a therapist who truly cares about you, not one who just gives you medication and ignores you. If you're ever going to find peace of mind and happiness, you'll need to find a therapist who understands you—one who can empathize with your . . . with your situation." Ariel nodded empathically, but Beatrice only stared at me with her cold, secretive eyes, as though thinking, "You stupid shithead." The more she stared at me, the more I heard myself spouting out advice—something I ordinarily do not do. I found myself wanting to please her, to win her over. I thought of that old saying "if looks could kill . . ." So menacing were Beatrice's eyes that for a moment my body tensed up; my lips seemed to tighten and my words came out of the corner of my mouth with a funny sound. I found myself monitoring everything I was saying, imaging she saw me as an arrogant male therapist and trying to act unarrogant and unmale. Then I caught myself doing this and stopped. "Excuse me, I think it's a little hot in here. Are you hot? I'll turn down the radiator." I swiveled around in the chair and reached over to the radiator. I took a minute to compose myself. When

I felt better, I asked Beatrice, "What do you think about what I've just said?"

"It all sounds very true," she answered softly, looking at me with her contemptuous blue eyes.

"We'll discuss it," Ariel said, "and let you know."

She looked at Beatrice and Beatrice looked at her. They looked at each other for a bit longer than a normal moment.

After they had left I sat in my chair pondering what had happened. What was it that gave certain people an unspoken power over others, simply through facial gestures or body language? From the moment Ariel had walked into my office, she had had that power. Of all the patients I had ever treated, she was one of the most powerful. When she was lying on my couch, I could feel currents of electricity in my own body. Yes, she was a beautiful young woman, but there were many beautiful young women who did not charge the atmosphere with their presence, beauties who were unsure of their beauty or who were conceited about it or who were of a schizoid disposition. It was more than Ariel's beauty; it was also her rage and how that rage got channeled into a determined, unspoken effort to make others feel her presence.

Beatrice had that same determination to have her presence felt. And, in addition, her force field had a more sinister effect, due to the subtle furtiveness and contempt that emanated from her eyes. The combined force field of the two young women had produced an emotional contagion. But this emotional contagion was more than just their desire to have an emotional effect on others. There was also a projective identification by which they divested others with their own rage, perceived others as monsters and themselves as the clever pair who saw through the veiled monstrosity of others. During the time they had been in my office, I had begun to feel as though I were being a monster of a sort—that is, a male chauvinist therapist with evil intentions. And I had found myself trying to prove to them—especially to Beatrice—that I was a good man with good intentions. Hence, for a moment I had caught their "disease" and was controlled by their unspoken thoughts and feelings.

This, of course, was also what they both wanted to do: they wanted to contaminate me and others with their own rage. They wanted us to feel and be what people accused them of being. It was a kind of turning of tables through witchcraft and, indeed, a form of behavior that formerly might have gotten them tried as witches. Today, they were simply wayward teens, modern youth in search of meaning in a decaying world; perhaps they were typical of some members of what has been called Generation X.

And yet I saw signs of hope. Ariel had brought Beatrice in to see me, or to get a recommendation for a therapist. She was in the process of separating from Beatrice (and from her mother), and she was perhaps coming to understand that witchcraft was not ultimately going to be the way out of her dilemma. It had been the way of her mother and perhaps her mother's mother, but she would be—so it appeared—the one who broke the chain. She seemed to be a little less disturbed than Beatrice: still under her influence, but moving away.

She came to the next session early and sat restlessly in the waiting room. When I opened the door she smiled resignedly.

"I don't think Beatrice will be able to work with you. I think you'd better refer her to somebody else."

"Why is that?"

"After we left here, we started making fun of you, as we always do of men we know. And I think if we both worked with you, we'd just make fun of you until you'd become ridiculous in our eyes, and the therapy would fall apart."

"I see. Thanks, I appreciate your honesty. So, what did you make fun of?"

"Oh, nothing important. For example, Beatrice made fun of your use of the word *happiness.*"

"What about happiness?"

"Beatrice says happiness has two *p*'s."

"So?"

"It's an 'in' joke." She lay back on the couch, playing with her belt buckle, gazing at the far wall. "Don't take it personally. We do it to all the men we meet. They all get angry at us. Michael, the man I've been seeing, got angry and walked out on us the other day. I don't know. Maybe Beatrice is a bad influence on me. Do you think she is? The doctors at Bellevue thought we had a *folie à deux,* they thought we were both crazy. And some of my friends tell me privately that the parts of the novel that Beatrice wrote are sick. You know, angry in a pathological, rather than an artistic way. What do you think? Am I making sense?"

"Go on."

"She's even angrier at men than I am, if you can believe that. Last summer we spent three months driving across the United States, and I don't think I've ever felt freer or happier than I did then. Still, I had this odd feeling the whole time I was with her, like something wasn't quite right."

"What was that trip like?"

"It was amazing. We drove and drove from New York to California without ever stopping to spend the night anywhere. I can still remember the flatlands of Texas as if I were there now. In the flatlands you could see for miles around, the fields were covered with bluebonnets, as far as you could see there were these incredible bluebonnets."

"Tell me about it."

Two women riding down the highway. On both sides of the road the flat land spreads out toward the sky. Before and behind them miles of glistening asphalt. Above them the cloudless blue sky.

"Hand me the milk," Ariel says.

"Hand me the ice cream," Beatrice says.

Ariel takes the pint of Baskin Robbins vanilla ice cream and scoops out a plastic spoonful. Beatrice holds the quart of homogenized milk in both hands and chugalugs it. They have been on a diet of ice cream and milk since they began the trip over a month ago. Their only other food has come from occasional forays into corn fields or peach orchards beside the road. They have stayed off the freeways, preferring the country roads that meander through farms and ranches and one-diner Texas towns.

Ariel likes the feeling of the cool, white ice cream as it slides down her throat on this hot day. She looks at Beatrice with fondness. Beatrice has a milk mustache, and Ariel pictures her as a milkmaid milking cows on the Minnesota farm where she grew up. Beatrice's face is pale as a milkmaid or a white angel as she drinks the white milk and peers far down the road.

Ariel feels good and safe in Beatrice's presence. It is easy to be with Beatrice. Beatrice always seems to know everything there is to know and to have an answer for everything that needs an answer. She is a genius, Ariel thinks, and she has chosen me as a friend, so I must be a genius, too. I always thought that I was a genius, but now it's confirmed.

"I feel so safe and happy in this car with you," Ariel says.

"Don't say happy," Beatrice says. "Happiness has two p's."

"But of course."

When Ariel and Beatrice laugh, it is almost in unison. Ariel wants to stop laughing, because she is driving and she is afraid she will lose control of the car. But whenever she thinks of two p's she thinks of two penises. She imagines the word happy *written out with two penises instead of two p's, two fat red penises hanging in the air like uprooted mushrooms, with large testicles at the tops as if the mushrooms had been pulled from the ground, roots and all. She looks at Beatrice and Beatrice wrinkles up her nose and throws out another laugh and Ariel catches it and they are both laughing again and throbbing. And then Ariel opens her eyes and sees something on the side of the road in the distance.*

A hitchhiker stands with his arm out. It is a man.

"Look!" Ariel says. "Speaking of p's."

"A male of the species."

Ariel drives about 100 feet past the hitchhiker and presses down on the brakes. The car jolts to a stop. Beatrice leans out of the right window so that her breasts rest on the window sill, waving at the hitchhiker, smiling.

"Hi, there. Where you going?"

"Lubbock."

"That's nice."

She leans out of the window, smiling gleefully.

The hitchhiker gapes at her for a moment, then picks up his suitcases and begins to walk toward the car. All at once Beatrice disappears from sight. She is giggling and bouncing on the seat.

"Quick! Quick!" Beatrice says.

"I'm trying!" Ariel says.

The car makes a grinding sound as it shifts into gear. Ariel stomps on the gas pedal and the car screeches off, swerving this way and that, running an oncoming car off the road. The hitchhiker stands by the side of the road, his mouth open, his eyes open, his ears open, his freckly face

*glistening in the noonday sun. Ariel and Beatrice race
down the road as the 1971 Mustang that they have
brought for $500 from a used-car dealer in Teaneck, New
Jersey groans and rattles from front to back. They turn to
laugh at the befuddled man, who stands in the distance,
a forlorn figure gnarled over two bags.*

"Did you see his eyes?" Ariel asks.

*"See his eyes? I could see beyond his eyes. I could see his
synapses quivering and flashing like lights on a pinball
machine. I could see his left brain pulsating, vainly
trying to restore his wounded masculine sense of superiority."*

*They drive all afternoon, singing Spanish songs and
eating more ice cream and drinking more milk and
gliding down the straight, flat country roads. By sun-
down the glee of the hitchhiker episode has left them and
they fall into thoughtful silence as they reach Lubbock.*

"Oh, God. Here they come," Beatrice suddenly says.

"Roll up the windows," Ariel says.

*The local males have begun to descend on them like so
many locusts in a dry season, whizzing by in their
customized cars, making faces and noises at them, hon-
king their horns, reaching out of their windows with fat,
elongated fingers.*

"Hey baby?"

"Where ya going, dolls?"

"How about a drink?"

*Beatrice and Ariel look at one another. Tired and
hungry, they allow two young men in a souped-up jeep to
lead them to a bar on the outskirts of Lubbock, where they
slide onto a splintery bench on one side of a booth. Both
young women are clad in T-shirts, sans bras, and blue-
jean shorts. The two brawny young men lean across the
table toward them.*

"What'll you have?" the first man asks. *He's the taller one, and apparently the leader.*

"Anything you like," the shorter man grins good-naturedly.

"I'll have milk." Beatrice says. *"We'll both have milk."*

"Milk?" the tall man winces.

"They want milk, Dude," his companion grins.

"Well, there's no milk here. This is a saloon."

"Would you like me to go around the corner and get you all some milk?" the second man says, rising immediately.

"Should this old boy go round the cob-ner and get us all some milk?" Beatrice asks Ariel, imitating his accent.

"Ay certainly do think this old boy should go round the cob-ner and get us women and chillun some milk," Ariel replies in a syrupy voice. *"And I'd also fancy some ice cream."*

"What flavor do you gals want?" the man asks, laughing appreciatively at their joke.

"What flavor we gals waaant?" Beatrice asks.

"Vanilla, I do believe," Ariel says.

The second man rushes out of the bar and returns in a wink with two pints of vanilla ice and a carton of milk. The taller man sits and stares at the two women analytically, wondering what tactic to use with them.

"You two are a strange breed," he says.

"Yes, we are," Beatrice says, *staring ominously into the suave man's eyes.* *"We absolutely are a strange breed. Absolutely. Aren't we a strange breed, A?"*

"We are living symptoms," Ariel exclaims, smiling proudly. *"We are living symptoms of Marxist alienation and sexual perversity. We're symptoms of industrialization and the deterioration of the human spirit. We're symptoms of the moral decadence of American culture."*

"We're symptoms of the breakdown of the nuclear

family and the corruption of the military-industrial complex. We're symptoms of the postmodern futureless world of leaking ozone and acid rain." Beatrice eyes the two men with great calm, scooping up some ice cream with a wooden spoon. "We're symptoms of symptoms."

"We're your worst nightmare," Ariel says. "We are the she-monsters of the male superego."

"We're polymorphous perversity personified. And we alliterate while we pervert," Beatrice adds.

"And don't forget existential dread! Certainly we are inexorably existentially dreadful!"

"Inexorably!"

"Irrevocably!"

"Indelibly."

The suave man looks down at the other man, who has once again slumped into the corner. The second man has a "don't-ask-me" look on his face.

"I've got an idea. Why don't we switch places," the suave man says, smiling, clapping his hands together, ignoring everything the women have just said. "Why don't you and I switch places?"

"Why should we switch places?" Beatrice asks quietly.

"So I can sit next to Blackie there," he says, referring to Ariel, "and Hal here can sit next to you."

"Why would I want to sit next to Hal?" Beatrice asks, as though totally perplexed by the request. Ariel clamps her nose to hold back a laugh.

"You know, boy-girl, boy-girl?" the man says.

"What's boy-girl, boy-girl?"

"I don't know," Beatrice says, smiling at Ariel. "What's the matter with us?"

"Gee, I don't know, what is the matter with us?"

"Do you think he'll beat us?" Beatrice asks.

"He might. Look at those muscles."

The young man gapes at them. He is getting very

annoyed now. He is a tall man with a crew cut and muscular arms that usually intimidate other men and impress young women, a young man who has probably grown used to having his way with local beauties, who was perhaps the quarterback of his high school football team and now works for his uncle's moving company, whose devil-may-care glint is rapidly fading and whose jaw is now tensing up as he flexes it. He stares at the two women as if to figure out which of them to slap around first. He is frustrated and he is worried. Ariel can see that he is worried, and she can see that his masculine ego is beginning to twitter. "I mean, what's going on?" he asks. "Why'd you agree to have a drink with us? I don't get it? What's up?"

Beatrice looks at Ariel and Ariel looks at Beatrice. They are both thinking about the word up. *They are both thinking the same thing. What is* up, *they think in unison, is the man's male game. What is* up *is his arrogant cock. And what is* up *is his cock privilege. He is just like all men whose arrogant cocks are always up, always up, up, up, and ready to exploit a woman's sexuality, and his game is the game nearly all men play, his game of trying to use his arrogant cock and his arrogant muscle to intimidate Ariel and Beatrice. Men always do that, but it does not work with A and B—as they refer to themselves. They begin to laugh and look at each other. They are looking at each other and only at each other, and the two men no longer exist, nor do the others who leer at them from the bar, and the bartender, and the bottles of liquor on the wall, and the smell of dried beer and stale pickles, and the sound of hillbilly music from the jukebox. Only A and B exist as they look at one another laughing. The two young men also look at each other but they are not laughing.*

"Where you gals from?" the second man finally asks. He has long blond hair that hangs out of his cap over his

ears and he wears a gold ring in his left ear. He has a soft drawl, and Ariel begins to laugh again when she hears his drawl and then Beatrice laughs, too. They are both thinking about his drawl. Ariel looks into Beatrice's eyes and she can tell Beatrice is thinking the same thing she is—that the man's drawl is idiotic, but the man thinks it is cute. The man thinks he is a cute, gentle Southwestern man and that ladies fancy his gentle drawl. He thinks of himself as a man who understands women and is willing to serve them and give them their space, unlike his pseudo-suave friend, but in actuality he is a complete phony. In an instant both A and B understand this about the second man, and they are giggling with much compulsion now and looking at one another, pupil to pupil. Men and their little masculine vanities; how transparent they all are.

The two young men look at each other again, this time with resignation. They sit back in the booth. The suave one runs his hands through his hair, then turns his head to one side and scrutinizes the two women. The second one sits back in the corner smiling as though everything is fine and he is just enjoying himself, tapping his fingers on the table and listening to the music. The jukebox in the corner lights up with rainbow colors and blares out a song about cheating hearts and downhearted women.

"It's cool," the short man says to the suave man. "Everything's cool." He smiles at the two women.

No, it's not cool, Ariel thinks. She is looking at the ring in the tall man's ear and wondering if he thinks of himself as an androgenous man who is incredibly in touch with his femininity and softness. She looks at the tall man and wonders if he thinks he is God's gift. She cannot stand either of the men. They are both so conceited, so full of male conceit, she wants to throw something at them. She wants to pour their Lone Star beers all over their hairy chests, which bulge out of their partially unbuttoned shirts. The longer she sits there, the more agitated she becomes. Suddenly she stands up. Suddenly she feels trapped. Suddenly she feels the rage simmering inside her, the rage that is always there like a reservoir of dark bile. She wants only to get back into the car and drive down the road, down the wide flat road surrounded by flat land where nobody can corner her.

"I think," she says, "I think . . ."

Beatrice understands immediately. "I think so too." And before the men can say anything the two women have grabbed their ice cream and milk and run, giggling, out the door.

"It's cool," Beatrice says in a lowered voice, mocking the second man.

"Real, real cool," Ariel says.

They run all the way to their car.

The car speeds down the long, flat road and the windows are open and they are sitting back and their hair is waving in the wind, flapping the way flags do on breezy, sunny holidays. It is the next afternoon and the sun is shining, and on each side of them are fields of bluebonnets, also waving in the wind. As far as their eyes can see the bluebonnets are waving and rippling here and there like a flowery sea, and the lifting scent of the bluebonnets baked and blown in the sunlighted air, stirred by the breeze, drifts in and out of the windows of the car as they meander down the road.

"Stop," Beatrice says.

Without asking why, Ariel parks the car in a grassy lane and they run into the field of bluebonnets. It is the largest field of flowers they have ever seen. It seems to stretch from horizon to horizon, over the little knolls and dells, across the prairie, along the banks of a distant stream.

Beatrice dashes ahead, laughing, her head back, her short blond hair bouncing as she runs. Ariel trails a few steps behind.

"Where are we going?" Ariel calls.

"Nowhere!" Beatrice lets out a buoyant cackle.

She runs this way and that, the bluebonnets up to her thighs, panting hard now and still running full speed, and Ariel can hear her quick breath and her own wind gusting from her lungs. The scent of the flowers is suddenly upon her and she is lost in the thick fragrance and dizzy in the sun that presses hot on her shoulders and the blue sky that is like a blue dome hovering, and Beatrice is running ahead like some fantastic galloping mare and she says, "Hello?" and runs in a zigzag pattern and raises her hands to the sky as though to greet the world. She says it again, "Hello? hello? hello?" and falls backward into the bluebonnets, laughing and lolling in the bluebonnets.

And Ariel trots by, lifting her legs high and smiling like a majorette on homecoming day, and she runs around Beatrice and she says, "Hello?"

And Beatrice says, "Hello?"

And Ariel says, "Hello?" and runs around and around, looking up at the sky.

"Hello? hello? hello?" Beatrice says, lying back in the bluebonnets and the Johnsongrass.

"Hello?" Ariel says, jumping over Beatrice.

"Hello up there? Hello? Hello?" Beatrice hollers.

And Ariel trots on and does not want to stop, she wants to keep trotting forever, and she can hear her legs swishing through the flowers and feel the cool grass caressing her bare feet and tickling between her toes and hear the bluebonnets hissing as they scratch against her

*thighs, and she comes back down the field and skitters
again in a circle around Beatrice, around and around,
the circle getting smaller and smaller, and then at last she
falls into Beatrice's arms giggling and they are both
squealing out laughter and rolling back and forth, this
way and that, tumbling over each other in the bluebonnets. And Beatrice unzips her shorts and tosses them into
the air and lies back in the flowers and she throws her
T-shirt into the air and yells at the top of her voice,
"Hello? Anyone there?" and her voice echoes across the
dell, and she is naked and Ariel notices that her skin is
bumpy with gooseflesh and all pink against the dark blue
and white of the bluebonnets, and her nipples are dark
red and stand out like beacons of femininity, and Ariel
pulls off her jeans and T-shirt and heaves them the other
way and the two of them are rolling around in the
bluebonnets, two nudes in the aqua blue sea of billowing
flowers, floating backward and sideways and foreward
on the botanical sea.*

*"Who?" Ariel asks, lying back to catch her breath.
"Hello who?"*

*"Hello, God?" Beatrice asks, looking up. "Are you
there? What do you think of your blue-eyed gal now?" She
wears a lazy, lingering smile of relief and ecstasy, lying
with her hands cupped under her head, her legs spread
out, her naked body open to heaven.*

"Do you think God's watching?"

*"Oh, yes, he's watching. He's probably leering. Hey!
Take me, God, take me. Take me now."*

*And Ariel gazes at Beatrice's lovely body and her own
and she feels herself becoming aroused and thinks: we are
two young women, two naked, beautiful, angry, gifted
young women on this day in the year 1988, naked and
alive and powerful as only a young woman can be, huge
in our angry blossoming femininity, basking in these*

bluebonnets in the proud masculine state of Texas, and there are just the two of us, and nobody else is here, and nobody has ever existed before or will ever exist again in all of time's stupid eons, and we are totally and amazingly here and our tender red lips and firm pink breasts are here and the nectar of our young angry femininity drools shamelessly from our flesh, and we are two against the world, always and forever. We are here now in the flatlands of Texas and we have grown up and we are no longer little girls sitting on our Daddy's knee, no longer little pets swooning in Daddy's arm, God no, that was a long, long time ago and it is gone, gone, gone, and I don't want to think about it anymore. Good-bye to all that icky-sticky Daddy stuff, good-bye to "Daddy's girl," good-bye to "Mommy's girl," good-bye to behaving like ladies while Daddy struts around the house like a borish baboon, good-bye to tea parties in the afternoon and mother's rages at midnight, good-bye to asinine little brothers, good-bye to gabby grandmothers, good-bye to overbearing nannies, good-bye to men who say "cool," good-bye to men who say "Hi, doll," good-bye to men who lie, good-bye to men who always need to be right, good-bye to gay men and drug-addicted men and weird Mommy's-boy men and men who stutter and men who shout, good-bye to it all. We are here now in the flatlands and we are the women you have told us not to be, yes, yes, yes, look at us now, Daddy, look at your little girl now, look at my tits, Daddy, look at my ass, Daddy, look at my bolsa, *Daddy, my* bolsa *is ripe and sweet and dripping with primordial ooze, Daddy, look at me, Daddy, look at your little girl who is no longer your little girl, look at me now, Daddy, LOOK AT ME! That's right, we are here in the flatlands and we are everything you hate, we are two sexy, bitchy, pushy, brainy broads, yes, yes, yes, Daddy, we have brains, marvelous, amazing feminine brains with cerebellums that go bleep and blip as they engulf and intercourse with the facts and fictions of the world, yes, Daddy, our brains can think and our pussies can fuck, Daddy, yes they can, Daddy, and we know many things that even you Daddies of the world do not know, yes, it's hard to believe but it's true, it's actually true, there really are some things that Daddies do not know that daughters know, some things that only bolsas know and Daddies can never know, ha, ha, ha. Oh, Daddy dear, up there on your pulpit of righteousness and disdain, seated at the right side of Sartre, the father almighty, with the great Kierkegaard at his left, up there on your Dadly pedestal contemplating the "sickness unto death," looking down at us mortal daughters of the world, what do you see now, Daddy so dear, what, what? Here we are, Daddy, take a good look at us from Mount Phallus for we are not dreading death as you would like us to, not at all, nor are we pondering the meaning of life, no, no, no, we are simply here, Daddy Dearest, we exist and therefore we are, and our tits exist and our bolsas exist and existence exists. Yes, yes, yes, we are here in the Texas flatlands and nobody can tell us anything about anything because we are young and we are ancient and there is nothing new under the sun, all is vanity, as somebody once said, and we are here, Daddy, two vain existential sluts in our prime and glory, the objects of men's desire and women's envy, more real than raw milk, cooler than ice cream, proud and raging in our youthful sensuality, smooth and strong in our feminine wholeness, wicked with estrogen radiance, and it's all happening now and we are here now and it's just us two women folks, with spite for God and man and country, as we lie strong and mad and free in the bluebonnets.*

So Ariel thinks and then she looks into Beatrice's eyes and Beatrice is friendly and smiles at Ariel.

And Ariel says, "Why hello! Fancy meeting you here!"
"Well, I do declare!" Beatrice says. "I never would
have thunk it! Never!"
And Ariel lies dizzily back into the earth and feels as
she once felt in her mother's arms before the earth rocked
away, and she laughs so loudly that a bird squawks into
the air, and then Beatrice laughs too, pointing at the
bird, and they begin to tumble over one another, tum-
bling over and over in the bluebonnets, two pink Venuses
undulating in the wide meadow, and she can feel Bea-
trice's heart beating and her own, hear the call of strange
birds and smell the pistils of the flowers, and she is drunk
and mindless and no longer knows who she is or who
Beatrice is and they seem to be one person, indivisible,
and she is no longer herself, no longer a daughter, no
longer a sister, no longer an artist or writer or thinker or
Chilean or human, no longer depressed or angry or
afraid, no longer here or there or anywhere, no longer
anything but a rolling oneness, a tumbling now, and
Beatrice is laughing or Ariel is laughing or somebody is
laughing and saying, "Hello? Hello? Hello? . . ."

"I never saw so many bluebonnets," Ariel said, lying back
with her arms behind her head. Her eyes were teary.

"They must have been beautiful," I said.

"They were. I don't know why I like them so much. I
don't know why I like the flatlands so much." She looked
around my office as if to find them again.

"Perhaps because you feel safe if you can see all around
you as far as possible."

"Perhaps that's it."

After she left I had a free hour and took the time to
review everything she had told me not only during that
session but in all of her sessions over the previous seven

months. The memory of the trip across the United States
supplied me with a vivid last piece of the puzzle, and I was
now able to achieve a fairly cohesive understanding of her
history and psychodynamics. I wrote the following entry
in my journal:

Ariel's earliest family environment was fraught with
aversive elements. Her mother, who was apparently a
borderline personality herself, was ambivalent, unstable, and impulsive in her relationship with Ariel. Her
attitude toward Ariel, according to Ariel's earliest memories, would shift from primitive idealization (Ariel was
a saintly genius) to devaluation (Ariel was a monster and
the cause of all her problems). Her moods would also
shift from briefly sustained optimism to bouts of depression and rage culminating in fits. Her mother also
appeared to have an identity disturbance manifested by
uncertainties with regard to her image and her career
choices (she kept going to school all her life to get more
and more degrees in different subjects). There was also
identity diffusion—contradictory self-perceptions, contradictory behavior, and contradictory perceptions of
others. She seemed to be frantic about wanting exclu-
sive possession of Ariel, discouraging her from forming
bonds with anyone else but her, which belied her own
deep fear of being abandoned by Ariel.

Her father was, of course, a co-conspirator. From what
she had told me about him, I diagnosed him as a
narcissistic character type with an highly idealistic self-
image (a false self), and he had to live up to this image at
all costs. Not only did he have to live up to this idealistic
image, but his family had to as well. Like many narcis-
sists, he was a high achiever, having become a cabinet
minister in the Chilean government. This idealistic

image was related to superego pathology—an infantile value system that lay stress on appearances rather than on substance, and rigid moral demands with respect to how he and his family behaved in public.

The father had formed what Heinz Kohut (1971) referred to as a "twinship transference" with his wife. He had a need to see himself as a superior, special, omniscient person, and to see his wife as his equal. They were elite twins who mutually affirmed and reaffirmed each other's idealistic self-images and overlooked each other's flaws. Hence the father had a need to overlook and, indeed, deny any behavior by his wife that did not fit into his idealized concept of her. Although he was not prone to the extreme ambivalence or mood swings that she was, he did have a tendency to fits of narcissistic rage if his idealized image of himself was threatened.

They presented to Ariel a united wall of grandiosity and denial, at times including her in their highly inflated, grandiose "club" and at other times excluding, depreciating, and devaluing her, projecting onto her devalued aspects of their selves. The result was that Ariel developed a borderline personality that combined the histrionic (hysterical) features of her mother and the narcissistic features of her father.

From an early age she began to dissociate from herself and to be unstable in her interpersonal relationships. She was never able to form a cohesive self with an integrated identity, and she was unable to stay in one place, keep to one plan, or stay with one career choice. Her mood, like her mother's, fluctuated wildly and included suicidal and homicidal rages. Although she had much natural talent and ability, she was able to use very little of it, for she was not able to concentrate and had but a superficial faith in her perceptions of herself or of others (a failure of ego-functioning). Her ability to defend herself (another failure in ego-functioning) was likewise crude, entailing primitive defenses such as splitting, primitive idealization, projective identification, denial, omnipotent control (the feeling of controlling other people through her provocations, as when she and Beatrice were provocative with men during a trip through the United States), and devaluation. Like most borderlines, she was not able to repress very much. Meanwhile, her father's narcissism created in her a need to be special and a pressure to live up to his expectations for her. What she saw as his hypocrisy (his narcissistic false self) left her feeling empty and always hungry for a real relationship with him or with another man who would substitute for him, yet she was invariably attracted to men who had, like him, false selves and who therefore ended up disappointing her.

There were two major fixation points in her early development. The first was in the late oral stage, the point at which her mother first began having rages and invading Ariel's room in the middle of the night. These rages produced a major traumatic shock from which Ariel never had a chance to recover, since there was nobody to whom she could turn to help her deal with the shock and soothe it. Thus, she had the feeling of being constantly under siege by the very person from whom a child expects nurturing. The second major fixation point was during the early oedipal stage, when she turned to her father for support. Instead of support, he gave her false support and disappointment, causing her to regress back to the first fixation point, back to a state of needing the maternal oral nurturing she had not gotten from her mother. Stuck emotionally in this late oral stage, all the rage she felt toward both her mother and father became directed at the father. She needed to protect her mother from her rage, for there was still a primitive idealization of her, and she still hoped to get the oral supplies from this idealized mother.

As she came of age, she sought to form a twinship transference with a man, one that would match the twinship relationship of her parents, but she was not successful because her ambivalence toward men was too great. When she met Beatrice, after coming to America in her early twenties to study art, she finally found somebody with whom she could do so. Her relationship with Beatrice was one of mutual primitive idealization. Like the relationship of her parents, she and Beatrice mutually affirmed and reaffirmed each other's grandiosity and omniscience and reveled in excluding others, particularly men, from their "secret society." Her relationship with Beatrice was also modeled on her relationship with her younger sister Florence. She idealized Florence and Beatrice in the same way. She saw Beatrice as an all-powerful, all-knowing primordial female, and hence as an object that would fulfill her own narcissistic needs. If an idealized object chose to be her friend, it was an affirmation of her own ideal image.

Her identity diffusion left her without the capacity to integrate either her own concept of self or that of significant others. Her experience of life was always subjective and ever-changing, leading to contradictory self-perceptions, contradictory perceptions of others, and contradictory behavior. Before meeting Beatrice she had gone from job to job, from relationship to relationship, from city to city. She was unable to truly empathize with or relate to others, having never learned to do so in her family. She tended always to misperceive others' intentions and distort even the most ordinary social interactions, just as her parents misperceived and distorted their relationship with her.

Through her relationship with Beatrice she hoped to find an ultimate resolution to the intense anxiety and rage that had overwhelmed her most of her life. Over the years she had sought relief from this anxiety and rage in numerous ways—through fits, suicide threats, anorexia, running away, withdrawal, going on special milk–and–ice cream diets, and bouts of promiscuity. When you keep doing everything you can think of to get out of a painful situation, and nothing succeeds, the frustration and rage continues to mount, and when the primary sources of that frustration, the parents, continually deny they are doing what they are doing, it is doubly frustrating and confusing. Her alliance with Beatrice—it was an alliance rather than a true friendship based on realistic communication—offered a last-ditch opportunity for her to relieve her pain. If she could not get her parents to acknowledge her pain and their contribution to it, then she would give them a dose of their own medicine. She and Beatrice would defeat them the way they had so often defeated her, and then deny they had done anything.

This aim of defeating her parents was not a wholly conscious aim, and she would not have been able to verbalize it at the time. All the same it had been a powerful underlying motif of her life. The fact that she was more interested in defeating her father had to do with her fixation at the early phallic stage of development. However, the underlying meaning entailed both parents; defeating her father meant defeating her mother as well, since she perceived the two as one and inseparable in her unconscious mind.

Ariel and Beatrice went on a three-month trip across the country that was basically a manic phenomenon; they were soaring on externalized rage and magical thinking. They had both regressed to the late oral stage—a stage of milk and ice cream. As long as they kept moving they were safe from the threatening world (upon which they had projected their rage). Their romp in the bluebonnets was the high point of this trip, the acme of their splendid duet.

As winter rolled toward spring the therapy fell apart. Ariel's sessions had become rituals of urgency. She did not so much do therapy as go into a holding pattern while her life crumbled around her. From the time they had returned from their trip, Beatrice had become increasingly incoherent, and now she had obtained a gun and run off, leaving Ariel to pay the rent. Then Ariel had lost her job, her parents were pushing her this way and that, and her latest boyfriend told her he could not tolerate her rages anymore. What should she do?

She used urgency as a whip to stir me and everyone up. One day the urgency was about how Beatrice had bought a gun and gone back to Minnesota to kill her parents. One day it was about how she was all alone in her apartment now and could not work because she did not have a green card. Then it was about how Beatrice had called and said she had slashed her wrists, and how Ariel did not know what to do and was afraid she would so something herself. Then it was about how she needed to find a safe place to live and was wondering about the idea of marrying an American to get a green card. Then it was about working on her novel every day and noticing that the sections that had been written by Beatrice were truly bitter, and that her friends had noticed it, too. Then it was about the many men who had offered to marry her, none of whom she could stand to be around. What should she do?

Each session she was harping on this theme of finding somebody to marry. Every other session she was informing me that she would have to quit therapy soon for she did not have any money. She ached to be back in Chile, then again she could not stand to go there. She longed to see her parents, then again she did not miss them at all and could do without them nicely, thank you. Each session she came in with a new decision about going or staying, all the while asking me again and again, "What should I do? What should I do?" When I could not give her a direct answer, she began criticizing the therapy and the therapist. "It's not working. We're not getting anywhere. You're just like my father." When I asked where she wanted to go in the therapy, she replied testily, "You're the therapist."

This urgency and agitation indicated that she was in the process of shifting in her attitude toward me. If I would not marry her on demand, then I was a bad therapist and I was not helping her. In actuality, she had simply stepped up the desire to be rescued by me that she had indicated from the beginning, only then I had been the idealized maternal-father and now I had become her frustrating, disappointing sexist-father. It happened so abruptly that I scarcely had time to adjust. When I did adjust, I was at a loss as to what intervention I might use to resolve the process. I realized now why she had left three other therapists before me and why they had not been able to stop the process either. Her negative mode—which she called her rages—usually sprang up like a spring storm. You could not talk to her when she was in that mode; there was no observing ego, and no ego at all. Only id. A more healthy person might storm for an hour and then come to his senses. With a borderline, it can last for weeks, even months. Perhaps, if I had been her real father instead of a therapist, I might have slapped her and shook her until she came out of it. Perhaps, like in those old movies, she would have responded, "Thanks, I needed that." But the range of a therapist's interventions is limited by ethical codes. I could not use any physical method. Short of that, I had to simply stand by and hope that the storm would run its course.

She began canceling sessions, then forget to call at all. Then she appeared suddenly and said she had decided to marry Michael, a young man of about her age. She brought him to the office every session for several weeks, and when I opened the door she would be gleefully kissing him in the waiting room. Then she would come into my office with a sheepish grin on her face.

One day, however, she did not bring Michael. On that day she strode in anxiously and sat facing me. She said I did not understand how desperate things were for her. Several men wanted to marry her but she did not want to marry any of them. She did not feel safe with them. The only place she felt safe was in my office. If she did not marry somebody soon her visa would run out and the American government would send her back home to her parents where she couldn't stand it. She glanced at me forlornly. I asked her if I should marry her. She said, "No, don't be silly." At the end of the session she said she had a check for me. As she brought me the check, she stood with her face a few inches from mine, looking longingly into my eyes.

"May I ask you one more thing?" she said.

"Sure," I said.

"What should I do?"

"About what?"

"Should I marry Michael?"

"I can't make that decision for you, Ariel." I stepped a little away from her, and took my time putting her check in my drawer. I knew that she was always manufacturing crises, and thought this might be yet another. Again, she had placed me in a double bind; no matter what I said, it would be wrong. And since it was at the end of the session, I could not get into a discussion about it. So I tried my best to sidestep the issue and put it on hold. "Can we discuss this tomorrow?"

She sighed, said, "I suppose," and whirled out of the office.

She canceled the next day's session. The weekend went by, and when she returned the following Monday she announced that she was married. She and Michael had done it at City Hall and she was quite happy about it after all. Michael was extremely sweet in bed and she loved Michael's mother and everything was fine. There was only one problem. She and Michael had no money and she would definitely have to stop therapy. "Anyway, therapy isn't working. I'm not sure it ever worked. I just need to get away from it for a while."

Soon after I began getting calls from Michael. One Saturday night I came home to find three messages on my answering machine. "This is Michael, Dr. S.," went the first one. "Could you please, please, please call me as soon as possible. It's an emergency." The second message said, "Hello, this is Michael again. It's 8:30 on Saturday and Ariel is playing with a knife. I'd appreciate a phone call." The final message was delivered in a tone of absolute desperation. "This is Michael again. I called you earlier. It's about . . . I don't know what time it is. Ariel just threw the TV out the window. This is a very big emergency. I can't stress enough what an emergency this is!"

I looked at my girlfriend and she looked at me and we were both shaking our heads. I sat on the sofa and Linda came over to hug me. Ariel was obviously upsetting Michael, and he was trying to pass it along to me.

I understood what was happening. Ariel was acting out the transference. She was doing to Michael what she would have liked to have done to me. She had tried mightily to lure me into this kind of relationship with her, so that she would have the pretext to take out her pent-up rage on me. But I had laid back and refused to take the bait, and now she had found a substitute object of abuse. She was acting out this ritualistic drama and making sure I caught every bit of it through the displays of passion in my waiting room and the dramas of high treason that Michael conveyed over the telephone. She had transferred onto me the quality of the relationship she had had with her father, and now it had gotten displaced onto Michael. On some level Michael also understood that he was receiving hostility that should have gone to me, and I could sense in his phone calls and messages a twang of resentment and anger at me. It was as though he were saying, "Here, you take care of this; this is your job."

While I was pondering this, the phone rang.

"It's Ariel."

"Yes."

"Did you get Michael's messages?"

"Yes, I did."

"I don't know what to do. I've got to leave the apartment but I don't know where to go. Michael's getting impossible."

"Where would you like to go?"

"I don't know."

There was a pause.

"Linda," I called to my girlfriend. "Do you know any cheap roominghouses?" I wanted Ariel to know I had a woman with me.

"Not really," Linda said.

"Can you go to the YMCA?" I asked Ariel.

"No. I can't afford it. . . . I could probably stay with a friend. I guess I could do that." Her voice had dropped a few notes. "Anyway, my parents are coming in two weeks to take me back to Santiago. I just have to find somewhere to stay until then."

"Can you manage until Monday?"

"I guess."

"Try to manage until Monday. I have some time on Monday. I'd suggest we do a session then."

A sigh. "All right."

On Monday Ariel and Michael ambled into my office grinning self-consciously. They were both inordinately cheerful as they plopped down on the two armchairs I had placed side by side. It was as though nothing had ever happened.

"You seem happy," I remarked, sitting before them.

They looked at each other and grinned.

"Are we happy?" Michael asked.

"I think so," Ariel said.

"So you decided not to move out?" I asked Ariel.

"No, I went back, but we're sleeping in separate rooms."

"Whatever," Michael said, shrugging.

I looked from one to the other. They were both about the same height and build, and I got a sense of a brother-sister undertone to their relationship. She had associated him with her younger brother, and it occurred to me that perhaps she had picked him from among those who had offered to marry her because he was somebody whom she could control. She had, of course, realized that whoever married her was in for a lot of punishment (just as she had considered what effect her rages might have on me, if she moved in with me). She would give her sexuality easily, but there was a heavy price to pay in mental torture following this glib sexual surrender.

As I studied Michael, I was struck by his sensitive eyes. He had the eyes of a boy. The very lightness of the blue pupils bespoke a boyish vulnerability, as if the lack of pigment in his eyes symbolized a lack of strength. He kept glancing at Ariel the way a boy glances at his mother for approval. He would glance at her eyes and if he saw that she was smiling, his smile would widen and if he saw that she was not smiling, his cheek muscles would tighten and his smile would fade. I also sensed in his smile a cover-up for the embarrassment he felt about having called me so often during the previous days.

"You don't mind not sleeping with Ariel?" I asked him.

"No. Not really. I love her so much," he said, beaming at her, "that I'm willing to do whatever it takes. If she wants me to sleep out on the fire escape, I'll get a sleeping bag and sleep out there. I'm determined to make this work out."

"He's very determined," Ariel said, looking at me.

"What can I tell you, I'm in love with you."

He beamed at her again, and she smiled at him and then looked at me. "He keeps telling me how much he loves me."

"Well, I do."

"How does it make you feel when he tells you he loves you?" I asked.

"I don't believe him."

"Why not?"

"I just don't. I don't trust it. There's something not right about it. Maybe because he says it so much. Sometimes I just want to say, 'Stop it, enough.'"

"You see, Michael, Ariel doesn't really think she's lovable, so when you keep saying you love her, she doesn't trust it."

"That's true," she said.

"I think she's lovable," he said, beaming at her. "I think she's very lovable. Only she just doesn't know it yet. When are you going to realize how beautiful you are? When are you going to realize what a treasure you are?" He spoke with enthusiasm and determination but not with authority, for his smile stayed squeamish. I had the sense that he wanted a pat on the head. Instead, he got a rebuff.

"You see what I mean?" she said to me.

"What?" he asked.

"Nothing."

"Tell me."

"You never say what you really feel."

"I love you, that's what I feel."

"All right."

"Well, I do."

"I think what Ariel's trying to say is that you deny your negative feelings toward her."

"That's it exactly," she said.

"I don't deny my negative feelings. I don't have any negative feelings toward her. I love her."

"But what about the other night?" I asked.

"What other night?"

"When you called and left three messages on my machine."

"Oh, that. Sure, I get angry at some of the things she does. But not at her."

"Like throwing things out of the window?"

"Yeah. I got angry at that. I get exasperated because when she gets into her fits I don't know what to do. But I still love her."

"What did you throw out of the window, anyway?" I asked Ariel.

"A portable TV set."

"Do you want to tell Michael what drove you to do it?"

"I think it was when Michael said I was just being theatrical."

"Well, you were."

"I was not."

"Well, it sure seemed like it to me."

"You see?" she said to me.

"Ariel, how should Michael act when you get into one of your moods? Tell him how you want him to act."

"He should take my feelings seriously."

"I did take them seriously."

"No you didn't. You were trying to be a therapist. You were trying to analyze me."

"I was trying to understand you. What do you want from me?"

"I don't know. Just say whatever you're really feeling."

"Would you like a suggestion?" I asked him.

"What suggestion?"

"Next time tell her you hate her."

"But I don't hate her."

"Yes you did," Ariel said. "You just didn't want to admit it."

"I didn't. I hated what you were doing, but not you."

"I think Michael took some introductory course in expressing anger in which the first rule was to never say you were angry at somebody, only at their actions."

"Oh, shut up."

"Do you feel angry at Ariel now?" I asked.

"You know, I'm beginning to think the two of you want me to be angry at Ariel. Is that what you want?" He was glaring at both of us with his boyish eyes, but the smile was

still on his lips to soften his anger. "You want me to say I
hate her. Okay, I hate you. There, is that better?"

"Yes, that's a little better," Ariel said.

"Fuck you."

"That's even better."

"Did that calm you down when he said that?" I asked
Ariel.

"Yes, I feel calmer now."

"I don't believe that," Michael said. "Anyway, when
she gets into one of her moods, nothing works. No matter
what I do, she'll still throw that TV out of the window."

"That's not true," Ariel protested.

"Yes it is. It definitely is."

Listening to Michael, it seemed to me that no matter
what I or Ariel said to him, he was not going to change his
approach. His own pride had reared its head—or, more
precisely, his male narcissism. It was an insult to his
masculine pride that he could not handle his wife. For
Ariel and I to try to advise him on the matter merely added
insult to injury. And if he experienced us as teaming up
against him, he would be all the more defensive. I decided
to take a different tack.

"Have you ever had any therapy?" I asked him.

"A little. I had some counseling in college. Why?"

"Because I think it might be a good idea if you got a
therapist."

"You think I need therapy?"

"Not that you need therapy. But you certainly could
make use of it in dealing with your relationship with
Ariel."

"She's the one with the problems."

"It's true that she has problems, and one of her prob
lems is that she gets into moods and wants to drive people
around her crazy."

"Right."

"But how come you married a woman who tries to drive you crazy?"

"That's a good question. But I'm still not sure therapy is the answer. I mean, you don't seem to be helping her any."

"It takes time."

"I don't think we need therapists. I think we need a live-in referee to mediate our disputes."

"That seems to be what you're calling on me to do. And I can't do that. I can't be your referee or mediator. I'm Ariel's therapist. But that's another idea. Not that you should hire a referee, but you could do some marriage counseling."

"That sounds weird to me. We just got married and already we have to do marriage counseling."

"Sometimes it happens that way."

"So you're saying you don't want me to bother you anymore?"

"Quite honestly, it *is* somewhat annoying to get emergency calls from you all week, and you're not even my patient."

"Fine, I won't call you anymore."

"It would balance things out if you had your own therapist."

"I'll think about it."

Michael did not call me anymore after that, but Ariel continued to resist by making and canceling sessions, by threatening to quit therapy, and by asking me to permit her to owe me money for sessions and then canceling them. I began to develop strong countertransference feelings. Every week the frustration mounted, and every week the resentfulness grew. I started to second-guess myself, wondering whether I should have said this or should not have said this, whether it had been a mistake to lend her money, whether I should have just kicked her out of therapy. I was shaking my brain to try to find a solution. No solution revealed itself.

"Sometimes I don't know why I'm a psychoanalyst," I told Linda one night.

"I know," she said. "It's a demanding profession."

"It's a terrible profession."

"Not very rewarding."

"Torture is more like it."

"Some patients can be spiteful."

"They can be witches, bloodsucking witches."

Ariel had gotten "under my skin" to such an extent that I was continually thinking about her. This proved to be a problem for Linda, who, naturally, wanted me to be with her physically and emotionally. However, one night I managed to creatively displace my feelings in bed. I must say it was wonderfully gratifying. It seemed gratifying to Linda as well.

"What's gotten into you?" she asked.

"It's what's gotten out of me," I replied.

It had really begun to gnaw at me. I found myself worrying about Ariel and feeling more and more enraged at her. I knew I had developed a negative countertransference. I was considered an expert at dealing with hate—mine and that of my patients—and had even written a book about it (Schoenewolf 1991a). Yet, no matter how knowledgeable I had become, there was always another situation to be confronted with. Such was the profession.

I recognized that Ariel had an erotic transference toward me of the most annoying kind, and I reread Freud's (1915) paper on the subject. He noted that the erotic transference was one of the most difficult to resolve, and advised preserving it for the purposes of the analysis, while neither discouraging or encouraging it. However, he went on to add that there were some women with whom this policy would not work. "These are women of an elemental passionateness; they tolerate no surrogates; they are children of nature who refuse to accept the spiritual instead of the material; to use the poet's words, they are amenable only to the 'logic of gruel and the argument of dumplings.' " With these women, Freud went on, a therapist was forced to make a choice, "Either to return their love or else bring down upon himself the full force of the mortified woman's fury" (p. 386). He seemed to be talking directly about Ariel.

In all cases of countertransference one has to decide if it is subjective or objective. Were my feelings or rage and my alternating fears of losing Ariel as a patient and desires to get rid of her induced entirely by her, or was something from my own past being rekindled? I discussed this with colleagues as well as with my old supervisor, and decided that it was a combination. The feelings were indeed being induced by her, but my own need to be liked by her, to be seen as a good, caring therapist (my own narcissism) had caused me not to keep firm enough boundaries with her. My primary mistake had been to offer to let her owe me for sessions when she had threatened to quit because she did not have the money. She then saw me as a clinging parent and had no compunctions about canceling subsequent sessions and spiting me.

Having understood my feelings, I then had to determine what to do about her. I decided to join her desire to quit therapy. There was really no other choice. Sometimes successful therapy means recognizing that there are some patients who are going to play out their repetitive patterns no matter what. It means understanding that the best you can do for some patients is to relate to them for a little while, try to strengthen their egos just a little bit, and model for them a trustable and dependable authority figure. I was the first male therapist Ariel had ever tried. Before then she had worked with several female therapists, with each of whom she had prematurely terminated treatment. She was still not ready to become truly attached to a therapist, must less a male therapist.

Although we had done some ego-building (I had helped her get a more objective view of her childhood and her present relationships and to tolerate the intense rages that overtook her), her ego remained relatively weak. There was still much anger at her father and at men and its accompanying paranoia and splitting. There was still too much of a tendency to act out and only the most minuscule observing ego. Hence, when she acted out her usual drama with me, trying to seduce me as she did all males, I could not interpret this to her because she lacked the ego strength to truly digest such an interpretation. When I tried using more confrontational, expressive techniques, saying things to her such as, "You know you're really pissing me off right now because you're putting me in a double bind," she would seem to be impressed by my feelings and the acting out would diminish for a while. Then it would resume again. If, when she said the therapy was not working, I tried to get her to tell me about it, she would see that as my clinging to her and become annoyed. "It's just not working, okay?" At the point at which she began treatment, she was still very much intent upon acting out, not verbalizing her feelings. She wanted me *really* to be her good Daddy—not symbolically—to take her into my home, stand steadfast against her seductiveness and her rages and see them for the desperate cries that they were, care for her, nurture her, stay with her each night and rescue her from her mother's clutches, and then send her back out into the world whole and complete. If I could not do this, then she would move on to Michael or some other man. She was not ready to listen to reason. She was not ready for a symbolic relationship. As Freud put it, she would "accept no surrogates."

I had done as much as I could possibly do. Perhaps some years hence her ego would be strengthened enough by the work I and other therapists had done, and by her relationship with Michael, if it became stable, so that she could finally stay with analysis. Her unconscious desire to make me feel like a bad, incompetent father-therapist plus my narcissism had caused me to think I had not done enough, and that if I lost her it meant I had failed. This was the trap I had fallen into; this was what had given her the power to enrage me. Once I had made the decision to use a joining technique with her, the rage quickly dissipated.

How a therapist ends a relationship with a patient is just as important as how he begins it. Not only did I recognize that I had to join her desire to end the relationship, I also had to make that ending a positive experience. If she left feeling that I was angry at her, this would confirm her feeling that I was simply an exploitive father who was angry at her because she would not obey me and had made me look bad and feel like a failure. This was how her father reacted whenever she refused to listen to him. It was important to convey the message that it was all right for her to terminate, that it was understandable in terms of her development and circumstances, and that when she was ready she could resume either with me or somebody else. Such a patient, with a fixation in the stage of separation and individuation, needed to be given the space to leave and come back and leave and come back.

When she came in for her next session and said that she did not think she would be able to continue therapy much longer, I had none of the stirrings in the pit of my stomach. Instead, I nodded amicably.

"Perhaps it would be best if you terminated. As you've been saying, you can't afford it right now. Anyway, after thinking it over, it seems to me that it's possible that you've gone as far as you can at the moment. Maybe you *do* need to take a break.''

She seemed both relieved and puzzled. ''Do you mean that?''

''Yes, I do.''

''I really would like to continue. I know I need it. Maybe in a month when I get my green card and get a job. . . .''

''I understand.''

When we shook hands, there was no longer any undertow of seduction or provocation in her eyes. She looked surprised, respectful, and a little sad. I must confess there was a tear in my own eye.

''Good-bye,'' she said, and whirled out of my office without looking back.

She continued to call me sporadically for a few weeks, saying she was up for a job and would be coming back. Then, in the middle of July, she called to say that Michael had been accepted into a graduate school in California, and they would be moving in a few weeks. ''I want to thank you, though, for everything you've done for me. For both of us.''

''You're welcome.''

I did not hear from her for another year. Then I received a telephone call one evening and heard her sulky, articulate voice coming from the long-distance wires. She reported that she was living in San Francisco. She and Michael had adjusted to each other, she said, and they were both happy. He was attending the University of San Francisco and she was enrolled in the San Francisco Academy of Art. She also said she had recently begun to see a woman therapist. ''She's a friend of my parents who travels back and forth from Chile to California. Actually, she's also my father's therapist. That's right, my father, who always thought everything was caused by existential dread, is in therapy. He had a breakdown last year. And my sister Florence, remember her? She tried to commit suicide and is also in therapy. Even my mother's in therapy. It's amazing. My whole family's falling apart and I'm feeling better." I asked her what had happened to her and how she felt about her therapy with me. "I'm sorry I left so suddenly, but Michael was accepted into this graduate school and we were evicted from our apartment, and anyway we wanted to get out of New York City, so we just came out here early and set up shop.

"How do I feel about our therapy? I think it was good. At first I was confused, especially when you agreed that I should quit. But now I think it was what I needed. I knew I was trying to stir you up, like I always do with men, and I was relieved when you confronted me. I mean, I knew what I was doing, but at the same time I didn't know. I think the therapy also helped me to adjust to Michael, to stop being so mean to him. I still have rages, but not as often, and I'm not quite so depersonalized."

I told her I was writing a case about her and she took it in stride. "My last therapist wrote a chapter about me in her book on narcissism. I didn't agree with it but it was okay. My current therapist has talked about writing something, too. I don't know why all my therapists want to write about me. But your idea sounds interesting. I'd like to read it." I promised to send her a copy of the manuscript when it was completed.

Today, the topic of borderline personality has become increasingly popular, not only in professional literature but also on television talk shows. It is the fastest growing diagnostic category in our society. One of my colleagues quipped that we have a borderline culture, citing the rise of broken families, drug addiction, suicide, homicide, the decline of empathy, and the increasing tendency of individuals and groups to demonize one another (a result of splitting people into good people and bad people, rather than realizing that all people have the potential for good and bad, depending on circumstances). I think of all these things whenever I think of Ariel, but most of all I recall how happy she was when she talked about the bluebonnets in the flatlands of Texas. She did not have a care in the world when she talked about the bluebonnets.

REFERENCES

Adler, A. (1929). *Problems in Neurosis: A Book of Case Histories,* ed. P. Mairet. New York: Harper & Row, 1964.

Balint, M. (1968). *The Basic Fault.* London: Tavistock.

Bateson, G., Jackson, D., Haley, J., and Weakland, J. (1956). Toward a theory of schizophrenia. In *Family Therapy,* ed. R. J. Green and J. L. Framo. New York: International Universities Press.

Deutsch, H. (1942). *The Psychoanalytic Theory of Neurosis.* New York: International Universities Press.

Eissler, K. R. (1953). The effect of the structure of the ego in psychoanalytic technique. *Journal of the American Psychoanalytic Association* 1:104–143.

Erikson, E. (1950). *Childhood and Society.* New York: Norton.

Fairbairn, W. R. D. (1951). *Psychoanalytic Studies of Personality.* London: Tavistock.

Fenichel, O. (1945). *The Psychoanalytic Theory of Neurosis.* New York: International Universities Press.

Ferenczi, S. (1933). Confusion of tongues between adults and the child. In *Further Contributions to the Theory and Technique of Psychoanalysis.* New York: Brunner/Mazel.

Freud, S. (1990). The interpretation of dreams. *Standard Edition* 4/5:1–626.

_____ (1905). Fragment of an analysis of a case of hysteria. *Standard Edition* 7:3–124.

_____ (1909). Notes upon a case of obsessional neurosis. *Standard Edition* 10:153–318.

_____ (1910). The future prospects of psychoanalytic therapy.

Standard Edition 11:139–151.

_____ (1912). The dynamics of transference. *Standard Edition* 12:97–108.

_____ (1914). Remembering, repeating, working through. *Standard Edition* 2:145–156.

_____ (1915). Further recommendations in the technique of psycho-analysis: observations on transference-love. *Standard Edition* 12:157–174.

_____ (1916–1917). Introductory lectures on psychoanalysis. *Standard Edition* 15/16:313–340.

_____ (1918). From the history of an infantile neurosis. *Standard Edition* 17:1–124.

_____ (1920). Beyond the pleasure principle. *Standard Edition* 18:3–66.

_____ (1926). Inhibitions, symptoms, and anxiety. *Standard Edition* 20:77–175.

_____ (1928). Dostoyevski and parricide. *Standard Edition* 21:222–243.

_____ (1937). Analysis terminable and interminable. *Standard Edition* 23:209–253.

_____ (1940). The splitting of the ego in the process of defense. *Standard Edition* 23:271–275.

Fromm, E., Suzuki, D. T., and DeMartino, R. (1960). *Zen Buddhism and Psychoanalysis.* New York: Harper & Row.

Fromm-Reichmann, F. (1950). *The Principles of Intensive Psychotherapy.* Chicago: Phoenix.

Haley, J. (1973). *Uncommon Therapy.* New York: Norton.

Hoch, P. H., and Palatin, P. (1949). Pseudoneurotic forms of schizophrenia. *Psychiatric Quarterly* 23:248–276.

Kernberg, O. (1975). *Borderline Conditions and Pathological Narcissism.* New York: Jason Aronson.

_____ (1985). *Internal World and External Reality.* Northvale, NJ: Jason Aronson.

Klein, M. (1946). Notes on some schizoid mechanisms. *International Journal of Psycho-Analysis* 27:99–100.

Kohut, H. (1971). *The Analysis of the Self.* New York: International Universities Press.

Laing, R. D. (1971). *The Politics of the Family.* London: Tavistock.

Lidz, T., et al. (1965). *Schizophrenia and the Family.* New York: International Universities Press.

Lindner, R. (1955). *The Fifty-Minute Hour*. New York: Bantam.

Lowen, A. (1958). *Language and the Body*. New York: Collier.

Mahler, M. S., Pine, F., and Bergman, A. (1975). *The Psychological Birth of the Human Infant*. London: Maresfield Library.

Masterson, J. F. (1981). *The Narcissistic and Borderline Disorders: An Integrated Developmental Approach*. New York: Brunner/Mazel.

Miller, A. (1981). *The Drama of the Gifted Child*. New York: Farrar, Straus, Giroux.

Mornel, P. (1979). *Passive Men, Wild Women*. New York: Simon & Schuster.

Panken, S. (1975). *The Joy of Suffering: Psychoanalytic Theory and Therapy of Masochism*. New York: Jason Aronson.

Perls, F. (1969). *Gestalt Therapy Verbatim*. Moab, UT: Real People Press.

Rapaport, D., Gill, M. M., and Schafer, R. (1946). *Diagnostic Psychological Testing*. Chicago: Year Book.

Reich, W. (1933). *Character Analysis,* 3rd ed., trans. V. R. Carfagno. New York: Simon & Schuster, 1972.

Rosen, J. (1962). *Direct Psychoanalytic Psychiatry*. New York: Grune & Stratton.

Schoenewolf, G. (1991a). *The Art of Hating*. Northvale, NJ: Jason Aronson.

_____ (1991b). *Jennifer and Her Selves*. New York: Fine.

_____ (1993). *Counterresistance*. Northvale, NJ: Jason Aronson.

_____ (1995). *Erotic Games*. New York: Birch Lane.

Searles, H. (1965). *Collected Papers on Schizophrenia and Related Subjects*. New York: International Universities Press.

Spotnitz, H. (1976). *Psychotherapy of Preoedipal Conditions*. New York: Jason Aronson.

Winnicott, D. W. (1949). Hate in the countertransference. *International Journal of Psycho-Analysis* 30:69–75.

Zilboorg, G. (1941). Ambulatory schizophrenias. *Psychiatry* 4:149–155.

INDEX